Why AI Undermines Democracy and What to Do About It

Why AI Undermines Democracy and What to Do About It

MARK COECKELBERGH

polity

First published in 2024 by Polity Press

Polity Press
65 Bridge Street
Cambridge CB2 1UR, UK

Polity Press
111 River Street
Hoboken, NJ 07030, USA

ISBN-13: 978-1-5095-6092-9
ISBN-13: 978-1-5095-6093-6(pb)

A catalogue record for this book is available from the British Library.

Library of Congress Control Number: 2023941290

Typeset in 11 on 14pt Warnock Pro
by Cheshire Typesetting Ltd, Cuddington, Cheshire
Printed and bound by CPI Group (UK) Ltd, Croydon, CR0 4YY

The publisher has used its best endeavours to ensure that the URLs for external websites referred to in this book are correct and active at the time of going to press. However, the publisher has no responsibility for the websites and can make no guarantee that a site will remain live or that the content is or will remain appropriate.

Every effort has been made to trace all copyright holders, but if any have been overlooked the publisher will be pleased to include any necessary credits in any subsequent reprint or edition.

For further information on Polity, visit our website:
politybooks.com

Contents

Preface

These are busy times for anyone concerned with the ethics and politics of artificial intelligence (AI). As I add the finishing touches to this manuscript, there has been the rise of large language models for text generation (since November 2022); wild claims have been made about the supposedly catastrophic impact of AI on the world by tech CEOs and the "experts" who inspire them[1]; and in June 2023 the European Parliament passed the AI Act, claimed to be the world's first comprehensive AI regulation.[2] What is going on? Is AI a threat to the world? And what will be the impact of the legislation? AI ethics specialists are in demand. Public debates about AI mushroom everywhere. AI becomes the object of (geo)political struggle. Tech CEOs such as Sam Altman manage to dominate the public discussion. They lobby publicly and are received by the White House and by European heads of state.[3] Citizens and governments are told that we have to develop AI fast, otherwise others will overtake us. We are told how and how much AI should be regulated. We are told that AI might have catastrophic effects and that we should pause the development of AI.[4] Things are going fast and the choir of those who hype or doom-think AI grows, often boosted by the media.

In the midst of this turmoil, which is often created with specific political aims, voices of those who calmly and systematically analyze the impact of AI on society are often not heard. But doing that work is important if we want to use the opportunities this technology offers and use it in a responsible way. Focusing on AI's influence on democracy, this book discusses the politics of AI by putting it in a wider intellectual context and offers a vision of how to move forward. It is about AI, of course, but it is also and mainly about democracy. About how vulnerable and resilient our current forms of democracy are and can be in the light of powerful technological and anti-democratic forces. And especially about what kind of democracy we want. Ultimately, that question is about what kind of society we want and what kind of world we want to leave to the next generations. Do we go with the current situation or do we try to make sure that advanced technologies help us to work towards the common good? This – not short-term corporate interests or science fiction fantasies about AI destroying civilization – is what *should* be at stake when we discuss our common technological future.

Kyoto, 21 June 2023

Acknowledgments

I thank anonymous reviewers for their comments, which helped me to revise and update the initial draft of this manuscript, and especially my editors Mary Savigar and Stephanie Homer for their continuous support during this process. I also thank Zachary Storms for helping with the formatting, and I am grateful to all the people who during the journey of writing this book have suggested literature, have been conversation partners, and have offered their invaluable friendship and collegiality.

1

Introduction

A specter is haunting today's political world, and it's an ugly and dangerous one: authoritarianism. Everywhere democracies are under threat, including in the West. Whereas the late 1990s still saw a wave of democratization, today there are many anti-democratic tendencies, which sometimes result in a slide towards authoritarianism. A 2021 report shows that dictatorships are worldwide on the rise. Polarization is worsening, there is a dramatic increase in threats to freedom of expression, and 70 percent of the world population now lives in an autocracy, compared to 49 percent in 2011 (Democracy Report 2022). Western democracies are not immune to this trend. Some speak of a new world order, with powerful players trying to destroy the international order set up after World War II and the United States falling prey to polarization and "decay" (Erlanger 2022). There are also autocratization tendencies in Europe in the form of a lurch to the (far) right, for example in Hungary, Poland, and Serbia. In September 2022, a right-wing nationalist Swedish party gained more than 20 percent of the vote. The United Kingdom became politically and financially unstable after populists and later ultra-liberal conservatives rose to power. In the same year, far-right populists won the elections in Italy, and their leader Giorgia Meloni became prime minister. As is well known from history, anti-democratic politicians can come to power through democratic elections and subsequently undermine or even abolish democracy. In some contexts, this is an imminent danger today. Digital technologies such as artificial intelligence (AI) offer many benefits and opportunities to society. But they also seem to play a role in those erosions of democracies and in the rise and maintenance of authoritarian and totalitarian regimes. Social media are blamed for helping to destabilize democracies by destroying truth and increasing the polarization. AI fares not better. Today, stories about AI are often stories of manipulation, polarization, discrimination, surveillance, power, and repression.

Even if authoritarianism might not be immediately on the horizon, the risks for democracy seem very real. Governments and international organizations are concerned. The US Biden administration recently warned of the dangers AI poses to democracy, complaining that there are limits to what the White House can do to regulate the technology.[1] A European Commission website headlined "democracy in peril" in the light of a report on risks posed by current digital technologies such as false information, manipulation, surveillance, and the increased power of commercial entities on which we depend in this area and which set the agenda for our digital future.[2] And earlier, the United Nations High Commissioner for Human Rights warned of the impact of AI on human rights, rule of law, and democracy.[3] In other words, AI has come to be seen as a problem, and it's increasingly recognized that it's a problem for democracy.

Consider the Cambridge Analytica case (Cadwalladr and Graham-Harrison 2018), which involved voter manipulation based on analysis of big data. Millions of Facebook data were collected without people's consent and used for targeted political advertising in order to support political campaigns in the

United Kingdom and the United States. And the use of AI in combination with social media has been said to drive political polarization and to propagate divisions in society, which can then be exploited by groups striving for power (Smith 2019) – groups that are not necessarily democratic. The rise of the far-right QAnon movement in the United States, which has led to a violent insurrection at the Capitol, is a case in point. It seems that we risk being locked in our own bubbles and echo chambers, besieged by algorithms that try to influence us and drive us apart.

The program ChatGPT, a large language model that has recently become both very popular and ethically controversial, has also been linked to undermining democracy. Some worry that AI could get out of control and take over political decision making.[4] This may seem rather far-fetched and at least a matter for the distant future. But there is also the near-future concern that AI could nevertheless be *used* to influence political decision making. For a start, it could be a powerful lobbying instrument. For example, it could automatically compose many op-eds and letters to the editor, submit numerous comments on social media posts, and help to target politicians and other relevant actors – all at great speed and worldwide. This could significantly influence policy making (Sanders and Schneier 2023). It could also be used to spread propaganda – thus influencing elections.

Yet AI is not only being used to gain power but it also increasingly plays a role in existing governance institutions. Here, too, AI has been shown in a bad light. Consider the automated welfare surveillance system used by the Dutch, which a court halted because it said that it violated human rights and breached people's privacy: did the use of this system amount to "spying on the poor" (Henley and Booth 2020)? In Austria there was controversy about the algorithmic profiling of job seekers by the public employment service AMS, which was accused of unjustly discriminating against some categories of job seekers (Allhutter et al. 2020). AI court decision making has also been criticized for being biased. In the United States, the COMPAS algorithm, used by probation and parole officers to judge the risk of recidivism, has been said to be discriminating against black defendants: a report claimed that "black defendants were far more likely than white defendants to be incorrectly judged to be at a higher risk of recidivism" (Larsen et al. 2016).

In the meantime, AI also became popular with autocratic governments. Western media have reported that China has been using AI for surveillance and repression. According to the *New York Times*, its citizens are under constant surveillance: phones are tracked, purchases are monitored, chats are censored. Predictive policing is used to predict crime, but also to crack down on ethnic minorities and migrant workers (Mozur, Xiao, and Liu 2022). Human Rights Watch claims that the Chinese government collects a lot of personal information and uses algorithms to flag people who are seen as potentially threatening. They say that this has led to restrictions of freedom of expression and freedom of movement. Some people are sent to political education camps (China's Algorithms of Repression 2019).

But the use of AI surveillance technology is not restricted to China or even to authoritarian regimes. Developed and supplied by China, but also by countries such as the United States, France, Germany, Israel, and Japan, it is proliferating around the world and even in democracies. According to a Carnegie's AI Global Surveillance (AIGS) index, more than half of the advanced democracies in the world use AI surveillance systems (Feldstein 2019a). Even if such technologies are used in political systems that call themselves democratic, there is always the risk that they are used for repressive purposes. In 2020, Brazil's far-right president Bolsonaro was accused of "techno-authoritarianism" for creating extensive data collection and surveillance infrastructure, in particular the Citizen's

Basic Register that brings together data for citizens from health records to biometric information (Kemeny 2020). And even in Europe and the United States, the Covid-19 pandemic has been used to mobilize AI and other digital technologies in the service of stricter law enforcement and control of the population. For example, in 2020 Minnesota used contact tracing to track protestors engaged in demonstrations in the wake of the police killing of George Floyd (Meek 2020), and AI has been widely used to assist far-reaching population mobility control measures.

As we seem to be on course for the emergence of new forms of authoritarianism and totalitarianism aided by digital technologies, it is high time we thought about AI and democracy and repeated Hannah Arendt's question in *The Origins of Totalitarianism* (2017 [1951]) after World War II, but this time in the context of digital technologies. Notwithstanding differences in specific historical contexts, is democracy in danger, and are conditions for the rise of totalitarianism emerging again today? In what way do digital technologies contribute to these conditions? Does AI undermine democracy and lead to new forms of authoritarianism and totalitarianism – let's call them "digital authoritarianism" and "digital totalitarianism"[5] – and, if so, how does that work and what can we do about it? And more generally, and beyond the question regarding totalitarianism, what is the impact of AI on democracy? Is AI good for democracy, and if not, what can be done about it? How can we make sure that AI supports democracy?

About this book

This book argues that AI as it is currently developed and used *undermines the fundamental principles and knowledge basis on which our democracies are built and does not contribute to the common good*. After putting the question in a historical context and analyzing it, guided by political-philosophical theories of democracy, it offers a guide to some key risks that AI poses for democracy. It shows that AI is not politically neutral but currently shapes our political systems in ways that threaten democracy and support anti-democratic tendencies by undermining democratic principles, by eroding the knowledge and trust needed for democracy, and by fostering the good of the few at the expense of that of the many.

But the book also provides a way out. It argues for fully acknowledging the political character of AI and points to the need for public deliberation and leadership in steering both our political institutions *and* the technology in a more democratic direction. AI needs to be rendered less damaging to democracy and preferably should work *for* democracy. This requires (re)shaping the technology at the stage of development and integrating it in ways that support, rather than undermine, the present political system. Yet the book argues that such a change in political leadership and democratic technology development can only be successful if there is an adequate political-epistemic basis. Such a basis can be built by nurturing a culture and education inspired by Renaissance, humanism, republicanism, and Enlightenment, and, more generally, by creating shared knowledge and experience. It is argued that, ultimately, democracy, and AI for democracy, depends on the making and promotion of the common good, on *communication*, and on building a (more) common world. AI and digital technologies can and should support this project rather than hindering it.

Let me give you a quick road map of the book:

Clearly, AI poses serious risks for democracy, and these risks need to be better understood. After a historical perspective on the relation between technology and democracy (chapter 2), which shows that new technologies have often led to more centralization but also emphasizes that there is no determinism when it comes to the influence of technology on politics, chapter 3 analyzes the two main concepts in question: what do we mean by AI and – important for this inquiry – what do we mean by *democracy*? Linking discussions about AI to political philosophy and political theory is needed since the concept of democracy is by no means clear and uncontroversial. As to my own position, I distance myself from definitions of democracy in terms of voting and point to richer conceptions: I argue that deliberative, participative, and republican ideals of democracy should guide us in discussing the problem of AI and democracy.

The next chapters then focus on how AI as it is currently used and developed endangers democracy: I show how AI impacts fundamental liberal-democratic and republican principles such as freedom, equality, fraternity, rule of law, and tolerance in ways that undermine these principles – thus endangering liberal democracy and potentially leading to authoritarianism and totalitarianism (chapter 4). Following in the footsteps of Hannah Arendt and linked to contemporary work on the ethics and politics of digital technologies, I also show (in chapter 5) how its use risks undermining the knowledge and trust basis of democracy through the creation of power asymmetries, manipulation, the erosion of the distinction between what is real and fake, and the creation of epistemic bubbles. In the end, AI may even destroy trust *between* citizens and threaten our self-image as autonomous political subjects, which we have held so dear since the Enlightenment.

But there is no need for doom-thinking. This book is neither pessimistic nor anti-technology, and it rejects techno-deterministic views that see socio-technological developments as autonomous and beyond human reach: there is still time and room to intervene and improve things. After an analysis of the problems, I consider how we can fix this and explore constructive approaches. How can we make democracy more resilient in the light of AI? And, more positively, what can AI do *for* democracy? In the last chapters – call it my "techno-democracy" or "democratic AI" manifesto – I argue that we need to not only change our political institutions and regulate AI in order to make democracy stronger, but also *make AI more democratic.* The technology should not simply be taken as given; we can change it: the development of AI should be democratized. In chapter 6, I argue that this requires changes at the level of tech development and its links to, and is embedded in, democratic political institutions. Yet, in chapter 7, I emphasize that the project of democratic AI is not only about making AI more democratic and totalitarian-proof but also, less defensively and more constructively, about creating AI *for* democracy. How can we make AI that supports, rather than erodes, democracy? I briefly discuss some work that tries to do this.

Yet at the end of the book I conclude that redesigning our technologies and reforming our democratic political institutions is not enough. I argue that the project of democratic AI can only succeed if it is embedded in a new cultural and educational environment: a renewal of our political culture needs a Renaissance and a new Enlightenment, this time assisted by digital technologies. Moreover, democratic politics (and indeed tech policy) also needs a deeper kind of normative transformation. In the final chapter, chapter 8, I argue that if we really care about democracy and indeed about fending off anti-democratic tendencies and preventing the rise of authoritarianism and totalitarianism, we need AI and other digital technologies that help us to realize and find the common good, and to really *communicate* and build a common world.

2

A Not So Democratic History

Asking the question about AI and democracy may seem strange since usually we do not link the two terms. This is partly because we tend to see AI and other technologies as mere tools, instruments. We see them as means that do not touch the ends: our human goals and values. Many people assume that technology itself does not much have to do with politics and democracy. They ask: "Surely all depends on what you use it for? In what way is AI connected with democracy at all?" But like other technologies, AI is more than a tool. In ethics of technology, a common way to express that is to recognize the truth in the saying that "guns kill people." Of course, people kill people – with guns – but the tool matters in ways that do not just depend on what people intend: it enables and encourages the action of killing. Without guns, there would be fewer killings. The same is true for the politics of technology. AI is not just an instrument. It shapes our actions and our goals. It influences our society. It benefits society but also creates risks, which are often unintended and unforeseen. Certainly, its impact partly depends on what people do with it, but the political influence of AI is deeper and its political effects more "internal" to what AI is and does than is commonly assumed. Its political impact is not just about politics and what politicians do but is also related to what the *technology* does and enables.

Inspired by many decades of work in philosophy of technology, I have formulated this insight as: "AI is political through and through" (Coeckelbergh 2022a: 5). The point is not that AI is a politician or a thing on its own, but rather that AI, as it is used by humans, has political consequences that cannot be reduced to its intended effects and that radiate far beyond the sphere of science and technology; they shape our societies and the ways we govern them.

Consider again ChatGPT: it is not just a text-generation tool but is likely to transform the way we write, the way professionals work (consider, for example, journalism), and, as I suggested already with my examples in the introduction, the way we do politics. These effects are not always intended. Think also of the internet and how it has already transformed our societies: not only the technology but also its manifold effects had not been foreseen. In this sense, AI is not just used by politicians but is itself also political.

This approach, which will be assumed and unpacked throughout this book, allows us to ask the question: In what political direction does AI push us? Does it make the world less democratic and more authoritarian, and if so, does that mean that we are helplessly delivered to its historical forces? Is techno-authoritarianism inevitable?

To better understand the problem regarding AI and democracy, to show how AI and problems with democracy have more to do with each other than expected, and to further discuss the question whether technology determines politics, I propose to put these issues in historical perspective (including some history of ideas) and reflect on the more general relation between technology and democracy.

Politics and cybernetics

Let's start with ancient philosophy. When talking about the art and science of governing the state in the *Republic* (1997: 488a–489e), Plato compares governing the state with steering and navigating a ship. He uses the term *kybernetes* (Greek: κυβερνήτης): the steersman or helmsman of the ship, the pilot, the one that is good, artful and skilful at steering and navigating. Steering a ship is a craft; it requires expert knowledge and cannot be left to the sailors. It also requires knowledge of navigation, for example, knowledge of the stars. Similarly, statesmen, Plato argues, should learn the art and science of steering the ship of the state: it is also a matter of cybernetics. They should know how to do it; it requires expertise and cannot be left to the people, a bunch of ignorant, quarrelling, and often drunken good-for-nothings.

At first sight, cybernetics seems like an attractive and productive metaphor for politics. Our contemporary term "governance" is derived from cybernetics: it is about steering society. Cybernetics is feedback dependent and goal directed. The pilot has to continuously monitor the movements of the ship and adjust them if necessary to reach the goal. Moreover, steering an ancient ship required coordinating people, for example, coordination of the rowers. Today, navigation or coordination of large and complex political units, such as nation-states and technology-pervaded knowledge societies, seems indeed to require expert knowledge. Can it be left to the people? Isn't that dangerous? If politics is cybernetics, it seems that the ship of state is better off when experts steer it.

Yet today most people do not immediately connect cybernetics with politics. This is because in the mid-twentieth century, the American mathematics professor Norbert Wiener used the term for "communication and control in the animal and the machine" (Wiener 1948) – thus introducing the contemporary meaning of cybernetics and significantly influencing the history of computer science. Today's many machines are cybernetic in the sense that they are able to steer automatically, without direct human control. We already have autopilots in airplanes and, increasingly, in cars. Shall we also put the ship of state on autopilot? Should society be controlled as if it were a gigantic self-driving car? Shall we use AI to steer our societies and coordinate people in order to deal with increasingly complex local and global challenges?

That does not sound very democratic, and neither was Plato's idea of a steersman governing the state. As my summary of his view already suggests, Plato mistrusted democracy. He reserved steering the state for an elite, preferably a philosopher-king, or more specifically, a class of philosopher-kings. These *guardians* would be virtuous, grasp the truth, and be dedicated to the good of the city-state. Today, that idea may take the form of guardians that use AI to govern nation-states. This is not democratic but authoritarian. It amounts to technocracy, or at least technocracy in its authoritarian form: the rule of experts. Based on this analysis, it turns out that both AI and cybernetics seem to be in tension with democracy. But what, exactly, is the problem, and is AI *necessarily* bad for democracy?

The question is timely. The idea that AI *takes over* political control may well remain a science-fiction scenario. But today it is increasingly used for governing. I already mentioned that AI was used during the Covid-19 pandemic, and often in undemocratic ways. In China, South Korea, Singapore, and Taiwan, AI was used to support mass surveillance and population control, for instance, via mobile phones that enabled police to track the movements of infected people. Even the US government has asked tech companies to access citizens' data (Council of Europe 2020). Moreover, decisions about the future of technology and society often escape democratic processes and procedures. The role AI currently has in our society has not been decided by citizens or democratically elected governments. On the contrary, AI and related technologies have been used to manipulate democratic elections, and the future of modern technology is usually decided in the boardrooms and labs of Silicon Valley. And this is not only relevant to US politics. Big tech's influence has global reach. As Lucie Greene put it in *Silicon States* (2018), today Silicon Valley is a "global powerhouse." The same is true for some other innovation hubs and for big tech in China, where the government plays a larger role in making the future. But the upshot is the same: tech politics is not democratic. Through their technologies, a small elite linked to a few global corporations decides how people will live their lives in North America, Europe, Latin America, Asia, and Africa. AI seems to be part of that tech empire. Is AI an enemy of democracy, as the history of the concept of cybernetics suggests? How resilient is democracy in the face of AI?

To better understand the question, let us briefly look at the more general problem about the relation between technology and democracy. The tension between AI and democracy must be understood in the context of a longer history of problematic relations between technology and democracy, a history that takes us back to the dawn of human civilization. And it's not a happy one.

Histories of technology and democracy

The point of looking at the history of technology and politics is not just to show that technologies can be, and have always been, instruments for power. This is trivial. Technologies have always been used to govern people – even if we are often unaware of this history. Since ancient times, they have been used in political procedures: as Risse (2023) notes, Athenian democracy depended on the use of technologies for allotment, timekeeping, and voting (2023: 51–2). More interesting is that technologies also had and have had a wider impact on society, including unintended influences. New technologies enabled not only new forms of governance but also new forms of life. In ancient times in Mesopotamia and Egypt, metalwork, building technologies such as wedges and levers, the wheel, water systems, writing, paper, instruments for surgery, and of course all kinds of military tools were developed. Each of these technologies served a particular purpose but also helped to build successful civilizations and were instrumental in assisting the rulers and elites to establish and maintain their power. Consider also the Roman Empire: its centralized power was enabled by 50,000 miles of well-engineered roads, connecting the capital with the borders of the empire. The medieval Latin saying "All roads lead to Rome" can be interpreted as expressing this connection between technology and power.

It was not until early modern times, however, that the relationship between technology and power was made explicit in the light of a new, modern understanding of technology and the world. In *New Atlantis* (1999 [1626]), the English politician and philosopher Francis Bacon described a utopian society in which humans are able to control their fate and assume power over nature by means of science and technology. Modern science has been fueled by this aspiration. Yet power over nature has always been accompanied by power over people. The ancient civilizations used science and technology to tax and control people. Writing itself, so important in humanistic cultures ever since, was not a gift from the god Toth (the god of knowledge), as the Ancient Egyptians believed, or stolen from the god of wisdom, Enki, as the Mesopotamians believed, but was probably invented by accountants. The accountants and managers in ancient cities such as Uruk required the help of writing and numbers.[1] These tools enabled people to run these ancient economies but also enabled some to exercise power over others. Since then, these instruments of power have been used by all rulers. And as political units became larger, collecting data about citizens became more important and was used to control them. Nation-states, especially, are data hungry. Long before contemporary governance by data (science), nineteenth-century nation-states already collected data from citizens in order to discipline and govern them. In his work on knowledge and power, philosopher and historian of ideas Michel Foucault has described how the French police and the Napoleonic administration used these methods to generalize surveillance of specific individuals and groups to all citizens (Foucault 1980).

After that first nineteenth-century explosion in (big) data collection, today's developments can be seen as the second data revolution (Robertson and Travaglia 2015), this time propelled by digital technologies. In the 1990s, with the rise of the internet, e-government emerged: government services were delivered digitally (online) and digital technologies were used across departments. Later, by means of smartphones, massive amounts of data from citizens were collected and shared. Often third parties, mainly from the private sector, benefited from this. Governments also started to use social media to inform and communicate with citizens in an attempt to render the public sector more transparent. At the same time, this digitalization and data-based governing made governments more vulnerable to cyberattacks. But citizens' vulnerability increased as well. If the government has your data, it can monitor and manipulate you. And national governments are not the only actors who exercise power over you. Nation-states have been losing power; new technocratic powers have emerged, and they are in the private sector. How powerful are governments and nations still, when big tech firms hold much more data and know more about their citizens than their twentieth-century secret services could ever dream of? Technology has once again changed the social order and has been used to gain political power.

Yet when it comes to contextualizing concerns about AI and democracy, the most interesting point is not just that technology and power have always been friends, but that technologies have consistently led to *specific* forms of social and political order and organization: forms that involve centralized, non-democratic control.

The usual story about technologies and politics, which is still echoed in popular history books, such as Yuval Harari's *Sapiens* (2015), and goes back at least to Marx, is as follows. Early humans were living as hunter-gatherers, and this lifestyle and the related technologies went together with a more or less "democratic" form of social organization. As people lived in small groups, there was barter, and power was decentralized and shared among people – or at least among the elders. No surpluses were created and animals were living in the wild, so there was no sense in trying to grab your neighbour's grain or cow: there was hardly any stock in the first place. Perhaps there was no perfect equality or absence of rivalry (some hunters and hunting grounds were better than others, some tribes lived better than others), but there was nothing like autocracy: no dictatorships, not even a state. The very idea of a state only developed once there were "estates," that is, with the agricultural revolution. Once you create surpluses and you stock them, someone else can try to steal them or tax them. The main danger was now not wild animals but fellow human beings. Some people claimed to offer security, but they demanded obedience and goods in return. Power was wielded over others, often involving slavery and other unequal and exploitative social and economic relations.

In the meantime, the agricultural revolution increased the population, and larger political communities developed. Political power became centralized. Hierarchies were established. The Ancient Egyptian pyramids are not only buildings with a function; they are also metaphors for how power was distributed in society. In Ancient Egypt's theocratic monarchies, power was clearly centralized and hierarchical. The upper class of royals, landowners, government officials, and high priests ruled over a middle class of merchants and artisans, who in turn were higher ranked than the large lower class of unskilled laborers. Already in ancient times, this created tensions between the classes. Violence was used to deal with this. And as some states became empires, hungry for more land and power, further conflicts emerged. There was oppression within the state and bloody wars between states and empires.

And that story did not fundamentally change for most of human history. The city-states of Ancient Greece and the feudal systems in medieval Europe were still examples of centralized and hierarchical societies. Money was used and trade developed, which in principle is good for peace and prosperity – money is a very important, often overlooked social technology and communication medium. But it did not equalize social relations and could not prevent the many wars that were fought for land. Agricultural societies need territory. And trade empires need land to gather the resources needed for trade and for their expansion. This led to colonization. Huge colonial empires emerged: those of Portugal and Spain in the fifteenth century, later also those of the French, Dutch, British, and so on. Capitalism evolved, for example in the context of the corporate capital accumulation and colonization of Indonesia by the Dutch East India Company (VOC). In modern times, the technologies of the Industrial Revolution enabled a new form of social organization: modern industrial capitalism. This helped to open up traditional societies and facilitated an orientation towards the future (Beckert 2016) – the old feudal structures were destroyed, or at least significantly weakened – but also continued, if not radicalized, already unequal social and political relations. Machines were used to exploit workers and later to replace them. Again, there was struggle and war but this time for the means of *industrial* production (to use Marxian language) and the natural resources needed for it. The evolution of technologies once again led to unequal social and political relations. In particular, it led to the accumulation and centralization of control by states and corporations and what

Marx and Engels called "class struggle" in their 1848 *Manifesto of the Communist Party*: in the capitalist system, the oppressed and exploited proletariat struggle against the owners of the means of production. Gradually, democracies were installed, but their power was and is limited in the context of these overwhelming social and economic forces, propelled by the history of technology.

Is this history of centralization, repression, and exploitation by means of technology unavoidable? And is it true? The reality is more complex. In principle, it is possible to live in agricultural communities that are more egalitarian. In theory, it is possible to organize an industrial nation-state in a way that gives more control to decentralized units and to the majority (even if the latter is not unproblematic, I will note later that it can become tyrannical). This decentralization happened to some extent and in some places: today, many people in the West and elsewhere live in representative, albeit still largely centralized, nation-states, with *some* power delegated to lower levels. And perhaps the idea of less centralized agricultural societies is also not just theory. Anthropologist David Graeber and archeologist David Wengrow have argued in *The Dawn of Everything* (2021) that agriculture and cities did not always lead to hierarchy and domination. They claim that cities could exist without central power. Their interpretations of archeological evidence throw critical light on stories such as those offered by Harari and open up possibilities for imagining different forms of social organization. In other words, the relation between technology and forms of social and political organization is not deterministic. There are exceptions. Technology does not *necessarily* lead to centralized power, oppression, and violence. This gives hope for emancipation and social change.

Yet unfortunately the dominant story about technology, civilization, and centralized power is often upheld. Consider the more recent history of today's digital technologies and their relation to society. At first, the future looked bright. The new technologies promised a more democratic future. In the 1990s, when the internet became widely used, people dreamt of decentralized, network societies, modeled on the decentralized, network nature of the new technologies, in particular the internet. That sounds good in theory. The idea is still somewhat popular in California, where earlier positive attitudes towards technology met with the counterculture of the 1960s and 1970s and contributed to Silicon Valley's ongoing success story. It also lives on in, for example, Pirate Parties, which promote more direct and participatory forms of e-democracy.[2]

However, the hope that digital technologies will lead to more democracy has largely remained a form of utopianism (sometimes called cyber-utopianism or web-utopianism). What we see in everyday political-technological reality is not more democracy but a concentration of power in big tech companies who decide how we live our lives and autocratic regimes that use digital technologies to maintain and grow their power. It seems that beyond the tools of hunters and gatherers, more advanced agricultural, industrial, and digital technologies support non-democratic tendencies. The people that had to row Plato's ship of state were slaves. Today, most of us row the boats of big tech and autocratic governments, steered by digital technologies and the humans who use and control them. We want to steer. We want to steer our own lives and be masters of the new technologies. But quite the opposite is the case. We do not steer but we are steered. At best, we are in the passenger seat while decisions are made by the Googles, OpenAIs, Facebooks, and Twitters of this world. At worst, we are the rowers: we are the engines and the fuel of the new digital economy, creating the required data and handing them over to those who use them to enrich themselves at our expense.

These problems related to digital technology come in addition to existing power imbalances and problems with liberal democracy. They are not *just* due to technology. AI is not to be blamed for everything, as König and Wenzelburger (2020) rightly suggest. But when our democracies are already weak, the negative effects of digital technologies such as AI will hit harder. Weak democracies are less resilient against what AI can do to them. I will argue that AI amplifies the problems and, in this way, supports anti-democratic tendencies that could potentially lead to authoritarianism.

While this is never just a matter of technology, we can learn from these histories (and utopian stories of futures) that there are clear links between technology and threats to democracy. This is also true for AI, which in the form of cybernetics has links with non-democratic ideas, and which currently contributes to the mentioned histories of centralization and domination. This is not unavoidable, but it is important to recognize the problems from the past, the future risks, and indeed what is already happening. These histories show that technology has social and political consequences and that it is at least very *hard* to avoid these. From a Marxian perspective, for example, one could argue that as AI is accelerating the substitution of capital for labor, those with capital benefit from the new technological revolution whereas others are left behind (Kaplan 2016). Again, in theory it is possible to create a form of social organization that is different. The influence of technology on history and society is not deterministic. Specific norms of social organization are neither necessary nor unavoidable. Given the forces and developments described, social change is difficult, but not impossible. If we really want, it seems, we can create a different society. For example, we might reject the Platonic model and try to create societies that are more like the ancient, more egalitarian (proto-anarchistic?) communities that Graeber and Wengrow (2021) ask us to imagine. Different kinds of political community, different cities, different kinds of *polis*, are possible.

Yet often calls for more democracy and political change make it sound as if social change is only a matter of the will and of actions of individuals. Consider Obama's "yes we can" or contemporary climate activism, which appeals to the (good) will of individual politicians. This emphasis on individuals and on humans is misleading. Instead, I will argue in the later chapters of this book that, given the important role of technologies in history, the key to social change is not only human and individual voluntarism and activism (although some leadership is needed) but also change to political institutions and especially change to *technologies*. If we really want democracy, we had better create more democratic technologies. In particular, I will argue that we need "democratic AI" and even "AI *for* democracy."

To talk about "democratic AI" sounds strange since it mixes two different realms that are not supposed to overlap: politics and technology. But as I have mentioned earlier, such a conceptual (and indeed social) shift makes a lot of sense once we understand that *technologies themselves are political.* Throughout this book, the assumption is that technologies are not merely neutral instruments for achieving human goals, but also change these goals and the human meanings attached to them. The histories mentioned here support that point: technology has helped to change the outlook of entire civilizations.

When thinking about AI, this means that we must assume that AI is not politically neutral and thus also not neutral with regard to democracy. From this point of view, it makes sense to discuss and take seriously the claim that current AI undermines democracy, rather than just saying that some *people use* AI to undermine democracy (which is also true but trivial). At the same time, it must be recognized that humans are always involved and have some freedom to steer what is happening. Therefore, AI does not *necessarily* have these effects and can even contribute to enhancing democracy's resilience. Perhaps a new kind of AI can support social change and support democracy. More will need to be said about this. But what no longer makes sense is to hold on to the usual "AI can be used for good and for bad; it just depends how you use it." After decades of philosophy of technology and social studies of science and technology, and after considering the longer history of technology and politics but also after having experienced how the internet and other digital technologies have recently rapidly and deeply transformed the societies in which we live, it is high time to say goodbye to such a narrow instrumental conception of technology and its relation to politics.

3

What AI, What Democracy?

If AI is political, then in what political direction does current AI lead us? Given today's developments and the history of technology and democracy, the question regarding AI and democracy is often asked in a way that emphasizes the threats: the question is how bad is technology for democracy? This is also my starting point in this book. It is the starting point for my analysis of the risks AI poses for democracy and indeed of how AI is already undermining democracy. There is no doubt that AI can also have positive effects on democracy. For example, it can assist voters make decisions by better informing them; it can help to spot fraud and corruption; and it can be used against bias. Later, I will say more about how AI can be used to support democracy. But today it is widely recognized that there are serious problems. Phenomena, such as manipulation of elections, misinformation, filter bubbles, governments using AI to undermine the rule of law, bias against some categories of citizens, and power asymmetries between big tech and ordinary citizens, have given rise to a discourse about AI that problematizes AI in relation to democracy (Sudmann 2019). For example, pointing to the new possibilities for manipulation – "programming people" – and political nudging by means of big data, Helbing and colleagues (2017) asked in their *Scientific American* article, 'Will democracy survive big data and artificial intelligence?' Experts are concerned. Citizens are concerned. Politicians are concerned. Is democracy in danger, and if so, why exactly, and what can be done about it?

The answer to the question I asked in the beginning – does AI undermine democracy? – will be "Yes, it does, and if we fail to address this our democracies won't survive in their current form, but we can do something about it." But before answering, we first need to analyze the question: What do we mean by democracy? And by AI?

Artificial intelligence (AI)

For a start, AI can mean a lot of things. Technically, it can refer to an algorithm based on human reasoning and expertise that makes recommendations with a decision tree, applying "IF . . . THEN . . ." reasoning to the input from the user. This knowledge is put into the system by humans: human experts in the particular domain. Consider medical expert systems: you enter the symptoms, and based on the knowledge that human experts previously put it in the system, the computer can reason its way to a recommendation of a diagnosis. This is so-called "Good Old-Fashioned AI" (GOFAI). It is rule based, and the rules are put in by human experts. The advantage of this approach is that it makes for very transparent systems: anyone who has access to the rules understands what the AI system is doing. It was especially prominent in the 1980s. However, this kind of AI was criticized by philosopher Hubert Dreyfus (1972) for failing to fully capture human intelligence and expertise. He argued, among other things, that the human mind is not a computer and not all knowledge can be formalized. Much earlier, computer pioneer Alan Turing (1950) had already pointed to the limitations of rule-based systems.

Yet Dreyfus's criticism was relevant since, from the beginnings of artificial intelligence – notably the Dartmouth workshop of 1956 where people such as Minsky, McCarthy, Shannon, and Simon discussed the future of computing[1] – AI was linked to the project simulating human intelligence. Today, there are still some researchers who work on so-called "strong AI" or "artificial general intelligence" (AGI), which aims to replicate human functions. Some believe that AI could have sentience or consciousness in the future. The discussion about AI often remains linked to (hijacked by?) this kind of project. For example, the question has been raised again after the success of language models such as ChatGPT. AI gets increasingly better at mimicking human intelligence, even if it does not have AGI and lacks intelligence of its own (which raises doubts about the appropriateness of the very term "artificial intelligence" and about the Dartmouth way of framing the challenges).

What *does* exist already, however, is AI that is very good in specific tasks (so-called "weak" or "narrow" AI). Such applications of AI are becoming ubiquitous. AI is used in chess and other games such as Go and bridge, where it has achieved spectacular results,[2] but also for instance in chatbots, search engines, text generators, autonomous vehicles, personalized online shopping, music and video recommendation, spam filters, detection of diseases, and bots in computer games. These are good times for AI. AI is part of our daily world, often without us realizing it.

Such AI is often no longer (mainly) rule based. Today, AI usually refers to machine learning: based on statistics, the system discerns patterns in (usually a lot of) data. This can then be used to classify and recommend. The previously mentioned search engines, chatbots, text generators, and so on are machine-learning systems, some to a significant degree. Consider also the medical sector: from analyzing thousands of images of lungs, AI can "learn" to tell if there is a high probability that a person has lung cancer. This is called image recognition. The system learns what (patterns in) visual data correlate with lung cancer. The same technology can be used for security and surveillance, for recommending videos, or for recognizing images of cats, for that matter. In the political sphere, AI can feed on millions of text data scraped from social network sites and create political profiles of people. It can tell with a high probability that you are politically left, for example. This information can then be used by political campaigns and even to manipulate your voting. Imagine that the algorithm figures out you're a so-called "swing voter" in a political system dominated by two parties: one time you vote for party A, another time for party B. This is interesting for politicians: these are the people that make a difference in an election, and therefore it is worth spending money on trying to influence their voting behavior, for instance by targeting them with specific political propaganda on the same social network.

But "AI" is not one thing (if a thing at all): it is not just the algorithm but also the data. It is not just software but is also linked to hardware and to the resources needed to produce it. It is about technology but also about infrastructure, economy, and ecology. Because of this relational nature, it is important for the ethics and politics of AI to consider this wider picture. For example, the use of AI and data has significant environmental and ecological consequences. As Kate Crawford has argued in *Atlas of AI* (2021), AI has a lot of hidden costs, impacting the planet though its energy use and the natural resources needed. AI also contributes to carbon emissions. AI, like all digital technologies, seems clean and virtual as opposed to the technologies of the Industrial Revolution. But this is misleading. AI could boost the economy, but at what environmental price? Or can AI help us to mitigate climate change?

Furthermore, AI is more than a technical system and is not just a matter of innovation and economy. AI is also about humans and their culture. AI is also the narratives we tell about it, the people and organizations that use it, and the meanings we give to it. AI is not only about data and computers but also about our collective hopes and dreams. It is a synonym for humanity's biggest aspirations and fears. AI is about us.

For example, the already mentioned idea of building human-like intelligence is for some a dream, for others a nightmare. According to some, it could turn out both ways, depending on how we develop and manage it. Nick Bostrom has argued in his book *Superintelligence* (2014) that human-level AI will arrive and that, once this happens, superintelligent machines will soon emerge, which will surpass human brains in capacity, will be difficult to control, and will likely replace humans. AI is then about the history and future of humanity. Transhumanists such as Bostrom are sympathetic to the idea that the end of humanity as we know it is near, whereas critics warn us about what they see as a dystopian "Brave New World." Others talk about AI in a more concrete, personal, and social, though not less existentially relevant, way: they are afraid that they will lose their jobs when AI takes over. Still others see AI mainly as a business opportunity. Or they hope that AI will improve . . . democracy. When people discuss the ethics and politics of AI, it is because "AI" touches upon themes and challenges that are important for us today. AI is not only about technologies, but also about us as persons, as societies, and as humanity. AI is about our values and goals. AI is about our future and about what future we want.

Democracy

Democracy can also mean a lot of things. It literally means rule (*kratos*) by the people (*demos*), but there are many ideas about what that means. In its "thinnest" form, democracy is simply a vote-aggregation procedure, in particular majority voting: instead of having one person decide, you ask people to vote, and the majority of the votes wins. Democracy is then a form of government in which a majority-voting procedure is used to make the important political decisions. Today, however, this is not done directly. Most of us are not asked to vote with regard to particular political issues. Instead, in most existing liberal democracies, citizens are represented by politicians, who vote on our behalf in parliament: this is representative democracy. Citizens are then required to vote for politicians once every so many months or years. But in principle there are also forms of direct democracy, in which citizens vote about decisions themselves, without intermediaries. This is sometimes used on a smaller scale: in city-states like ancient Athens (although many people were excluded from voting) or in small nations and regions, like Switzerland. Jean-Jacques Rousseau, one of the main theorists of democracy, developed his ideas in the context of the (then) city-state of Geneva in the eighteenth century. Influenced by republicanism as it developed in ancient times and the Renaissance, he argued that power should be in the hands of the people, preferably in the form of a direct democracy. Here, democracy is not about voting as a count of individual opinions but about *res publica*, about public affairs and the common good.

This leads us to "thicker" conceptions of democracy, which have governments ask more from their citizens than to vote. This is especially true for those democracy theories that emerged in the tradition of republicanism and in Enlightenment thinking influenced by that tradition. Classical republicanism, as first developed in Ancient Greece and Rome, was a view of politics and government that emphasized self-rule and the participation of citizens (as opposed to authoritarian rule by kings and emperors, for example). But it also introduced other ideas that "thicken" and enrich this conception of democracy, such as civic virtue and education, and the common good. In philosophical republicanism from Aristotle to Rousseau, citizens were not only given the right to vote but were also supposed to be good citizens and to care about, and contribute to, the common good.

Today's deliberative and participative democracy theories put less emphasis on ethics and virtue but keep the idea that citizens play an active political role (participation and deliberation rather than just voting), with some normative orientation to the common good. Interestingly, these theories allow but also *require* people to think about and promote the common good and to participate in decision making, not just by voting but also by deliberating and discussing how the state should be steered (Cohen 1986; Estlund 2009; Habermas 1990; Landemore 2020). Thus, in these views, democracy is more than a vote-aggregation algorithm, let alone just an expression of opinion on social media. Instead, it requires active participation. It presupposes a view of citizens as autonomous Enlightenment subjects who reason and discuss what is best for society, who are willing to render their own views vulnerable to discussion, and who are willing to revise them if needed. Inspired by the republican tradition, one can also use the language of civic virtues and civic duties, and speak about the duty to participate in society and politics. Following Aristotle, this can also be linked to virtue, in particular the virtue of justice. According to thinkers in this tradition, active engagement by citizens does not only prevent the abuse of power but also helps us to develop ourselves as virtuous persons and as political beings. This is not only a matter of nature (we are political animals, to use Aristotle's term) but also requires nurture: citizens need to develop themselves, and they need to be educated. Civic education is needed.

An interesting and important angle from which to look at these theories of democracy is to use the concept of communication, which can also be connected to the common good. According to Fuchs (2023), democracy is "organized as processes of communication where humans inform themselves, debate, and take collectively binding decisions" (2023: 12).

This requires a public sphere: a social sphere where people can freely discuss political problems and thus form a public and a public opinion. Moreover, in the republican philosophical tradition broadly conceived, for example in Rousseau, Dewey, and Arendt but also earlier already in Cicero and Augustine, there is also a richer meaning to communication in the requirement that when citizens discuss common issues, they put their private interests aside and care about the common good. In Rousseau (1997 [1762]), this takes the form of submitting to the general will. That's a controversial idea since it may lead to a form of authoritarianism: a majority or dictator claiming to embody the general will may impose their will on others and repress other voices. But leaving that specific concept aside, the republican tradition defends an idea of democracy that is about communication in the sense of having and creating something in common. Dewey and Habermas stressed not only participation but also communication. In *Democracy and Education* (1944), Dewey sees communication as a process in which participants learn to see the perspective of others and cooperate on shared problems; this enables both personal and societal growth. One could say that it leads to more community, understood as a coming together. For Habermas, "communicative action" (1984) is about the pursuit of goals based on a shared understanding. Arendt (1998 [1958]) argued that politics requires a shared public space and the creation and maintenance of a common world. These republican thinkers thus defend a more relational approach to democracy, which connects the person to the political whole, and an approach in which democracy is not only understood instrumentally but has intrinsic value: we learn to develop ourselves and we develop ourselves as a community.

At the end of the book, I will say more about these concepts, which together constitute an interesting and rich, thick version of democracy: I will argue that this conception of democracy can and should guide the development of democratic AI and

AI for democracy. For now, let me first warn for, and take distance from, a Platonic version of this view.

Plato emphasized that politics requires knowledge. The rich version of democracy I have just outlined agrees with this in the sense that it acknowledges that this way of governing assumes knowledge on the part of the citizens: they need to have knowledge in order to participate in governing. This means not just knowledge about political parties and their election programs, as in the kinds of representative systems we have today, but a far broader range of political knowledge and education. All the knowledge and skill needed for being a *kybernetes*. But in contrast to Plato's authoritarian political cybernetics, the democratic version holds that *all of us* should steer. All citizens should participate in political decisions. And in the end here, democracy and politics is about more than governance: it is about communication and about working towards the common good. This requires knowledge and understanding – something all of us should exercise and develop before, in, and through the democratic process.

But is it possible and desirable that *all* of us do this and acquire this knowledge? How inclusive is and should democracy be? In Plato's time, when these republican democracy theories emerged, only citizens governed since they could free themselves from work and labor. But that excluded the rest of the population; the class of citizens covered only a small part of the Athenian population. Arendt's analysis of politics in *The Human Condition* (1998 [1958]), which celebrates political action as opposed to work and labor, is inspired by this ancient, hierarchical model of activities, itself based on a hierarchical model of society: the ancient male citizens talk politics, while the work and household is done by others who were excluded from that form of "democracy": women, slaves, craftsmen. Today, slavery has been abolished (at least officially) and most of us tend to live in less hierarchical societies with lower levels of domination. And to her credit, Arendt rejected the hierarchical model. But the issue remains relevant. Is direct democracy possible when most of us are caught up in stressful jobs, exhausting family activities, and a demanding socioeconomic system and technological environment that leaves little time and energy for political activities? Moreover, today expert knowledge seems to be required to understand what goes on in complex knowledge societies, with science and technology playing a key role. This creates a challenge for democracy, at least in its direct form. Can and should *all* of us have this knowledge?

The traditional republican answer is: yes. But the world has changed. While education as proposed by Dewey and others is part of the answer (I will return to this issue later in this book), it is unlikely that it can entirely solve the problem. Governing modern societies is not quite like governing an ancient city-state; it requires a high level of expertise in a wide range of domains. And this is a problem for deliberative, participative, and republican ideals of democracy. As Zarkadakis (2020) has argued, deliberative models of self-governance face the problem of "knowledge asymmetries": there are gaps in knowledge between experts and non-experts. He puts the problem as follows: "Complex problems require expert knowledge in order to be solved, but in a democracy they also need the approval and consent of the electorate" (2020: xxiv).

Contemporary political theory after the so-called epistemic turn (Landemore 2017), and indeed all contemporary political systems that increasingly rely on expertise, hence faces the challenge to at the same time acknowledge that modern political cybernetics requires knowledge *and* make sure that the system is and remains democratic. One way to put this is to frame the issue in terms of truth. If systems go too much to the side of knowledge and expertise, they face the objection that truth can be tyrannical: it can lead to technocracy, or at least technocracy in its authoritarian form. At first sight, it sounds good to say that government should be based on the truth.

But can we be certain that a particular view is the truth? Who decides this? Perhaps there is no single truth. And there is the danger that one group of people (those who claim to hold the truth) tyrannizes and oppresses others in the name of truth. In her essay on truth and politics, Arendt (1968) argued that, seen from a political perspective, truth is despotic and domineering since it does not take into account other people's opinions. It belongs to a mode of thinking that precludes political debate and does not require imagining the standpoint of the other. If, on the other hand, political systems go too much to the side of democracy (at least, if simply understood as majority rule, what Arendt calls "counting noses"), the majority can become tyrannical as well, and ignorance can reign. The claim that no knowledge and expertise is needed for government also leads to disaster. Plato reminds us how problematic it is when a society is steered by ignorant people. Today, we see again the rise of anti-intellectualist (and anti-science) forms of populism; consider Trumpism in the United States. How do we navigate between these poles, especially in the light of AI? And are we even ready to confront the problem?

Here the analogy of the ship or the airplane breaks down. It is not possible for everyone to steer a boat.[3] But perhaps governance should not be like steering a boat in the first place. Perhaps it should not be cybernetics at all. Going beyond Plato and his authoritarianism, we need better metaphors, and to be honest, we still haven't found a good one. This is not just due to a lack of conceptual imagination; it is also because we are not yet living in a democracy and lack the full experience of such a system – if we agree at all about what such a full, realized form of democracy would look like. Paraphrasing Mahatma Gandhi's answer when asked what he thought about western civilization, we can provisionally answer the main question of this book with: "Democracy? I think it would be a good idea." When we ask about AI and democracy, it is good to keep in mind that democracy, especially in its richer version, remains an ideal that is not fully realized. We lack the collective experience. We lack it because we didn't really try it, or at least we didn't try hard. Partly that is due to disagreement about what democracy means. But partly the problem is that *we don't know* what democracy means and should mean today. We don't really know what we want. We want democracy and we want expertise, but we don't know what democracy means and we lack a clear idea how to combine it with expertise.

But if we want to know what democracy is, what about studying those existing systems that we call "democratic"? This is more problematic than it may seem. One may consider western democracies but, taking a global perspective, it is not clear that all political institutions in the world should look exactly like what western thinkers have in mind when they talk about democracy, say, the partly democratic systems that exist in Western Europe and North America. There may be alternative forms of democracy that are equally good. And are there "pure" democracies? The actual situation is that everywhere the forces of democracy and authoritarianism are subject to continuous interaction, negotiation, blending, and change. There are democratic and anti-democratic forces. There are blends and compromises. There are changes. Today, the direction of change is often towards authoritarianism, even in the West. Nunes Da Costa (2022) uses the term "democratic despotisms" to refer to tendencies to despotism in today's democratic contexts.

When talking about authoritarianism, many people in the West think about the past (Nazi Germany, for example) or about forms of authoritarianism in Russia and China. But problems are also closer to their home, where anti-democratic tendencies have emerged. Right-wing populism and the far right have made a lot of progress, even in Europe. Trump in the United States and Meloni in Italy come to mind. While such movements may not advocate full-blown authoritarianism and usually claim a majoritarian ethos (saying that they will do what the majority of the people want, thus appealing to a thin conception of democracy), they tend to pay only lip service to democracy and may well be all too ready to undermine it once they assume power.

Yet things get even more uncomfortable when we realize that the problem of "'democratic despotisms" is not just about authoritarianism; democracy itself seems to have some inherent weaknesses. In *Democracy in America* (2012 [1835]), Alexis de Tocqueville had already warned of the tyranny of the majority: without checks, one party can become dominant and oppress the minority (1835: 306–7). This is one reason why a liberal democracy needs a basis of individual rights to protect people from an oppressive majority. There is also always the danger that private interests of individuals take precedence over the common good and disable discussion in the public space – something Arendt and other philosophers from the republican and deliberative democracy tradition rightly worry about. This seems to be happening today in the context of AI, when private interests shape its future and when discussion in the public space is plagued by undemocratic tendencies, including the intended creation of polarization and attempts to silence others.[4] (I will say more about these effects of AI in the next chapters.)

Thus the reality (and slowly also the theory) is more complex than the democracy-versus-autocracy binary – it is important to keep in mind a global context with all its variety in political culture – and real, existing democracies have inherent weaknesses and challenges. Nevertheless, and perhaps also *because* of the mentioned phenomena and complexity of the problems, it makes sense to ask the present question regarding democracy and AI, with "democracy" understood as an ideal, which is realized and performed to various degrees and which can take various forms in the West and elsewhere. The question of democracy and AI is then relevant for all these different partial realizations of democracy, which (all) face anti-democratic (and sometimes authoritarian) tendencies and threats to various degrees and in various shapes. For example, it makes sense to ask if and to what extent today the United States of America is a democracy, and how its political order, including its anti-democratic tendencies, is influenced by AI and digital technologies.

Finally, there is the question of the borders of the *demos* and the *res publica*. Who is allowed on the ship in the first place? And if that metaphor was not democratic, then who are the people in "rule by the people"? Is this about cities, regions, nation-states, perhaps a global collective? And can non-humans be part of political communities too? For example, can animals be citizens, and should they be represented somehow? And how can we conceptually recognize the political value and significance of the environment and the planet? Is there a good philosophical argument for restricting the borders to a national territory or to humanity? Is an anthropocentric conception of democracy sustainable?[5] In this book, I will limit the discussion to democracies consisting of humans, but as I suggested in other work on the politics of AI, it is both worthwhile and desirable to further explore this area.

To conclude, when considering AI and democracy, discussions about democracy and politics that have kept political philosophers busy since ancient times surface again, sometimes also raising relatively new questions, such as those concerning the place of scientific expertise in society or the boundaries of the *demos* in the light of criticisms of anthropocentrism. As with the ethics of AI (or at least philosophical approaches to that topic), which continues to spark discussions about the meaning and nature of ethics itself, talking about the politics of AI from a philosophical point of view unavoidably leads us into long-standing philosophical debates about the basic concepts used in thinking about politics, in particular, discussions about democracy and related political-philosophical concepts. These will remain the gravitational center of this book.

In the following chapters, I will show how and why AI can undermine democracy (with the term understood as an ideal and as only partially realized in practice). First, I will argue that the problem is not just voter manipulation, but that there are also other and perhaps even more important and deeper ways in which AI risks eroding the very foundations of our democracies: democratic principles such as freedom, equality between citizens, fraternity, tolerance, and the rule of law, but also the basis of knowledge and trust needed for a richer, more stable, and more resilient form of democracy that can face the challenges of the twenty-first century. Next, I will argue that we can fix this, or rather, that we can mitigate the risks by strengthening and transforming our political institutions and by developing solid AI regulation, but also by changing our technologies, in this case AI itself. Based on recognizing the deeply political non-neutrality of AI, I will propose the development of "democratic AI": a form of technology democratization which systematically intervenes at the technical level. This is about using and *developing* a new kind of AI that not only protects but also fosters democracy. It is about AI *for* democracy. But changes at the technical level are not enough: AI development needs to be embedded in a new culture that is thoroughly interdisciplinary and humanistic. Since AI is not just a technical thing but also a narrative and a dream, I propose that we also further develop our political imagination and transform education. Here the arts and humanities, next to the technical and social sciences, have a key role to play. I call for a new humanism, a new Renaissance, and a new Enlightenment. The main point is that the future of democracy and AI should not be left to either tech experts or professional politicians. If we take democracy seriously, then what AI is and becomes should be shaped by all of us. But this requires knowledge, imagination, education, and – as I will argue in the last chapter – *communication* and an orientation to the *common good.*

4

How AI Undermines the Basic Principles of Democracy

In March 2018, a whistleblower revealed to the press how a political consulting firm harvested more than 50 million Facebook voter profiles to predict and influence voting in the US elections. The company, Cambridge Analytica, worked for Donald Trump's election team and was at the time headed by Steve Bannon, Trump's main advisor. The scandal was not only the harvesting of so much data without people's consent, but also that these data were then used to influence voting behavior. In the whistleblower's own words: "We exploited Facebook to harvest millions of people's profiles. And built models to exploit what we knew about them and target their inner demons" (Cadwalladr and Graham-Harrison 2018). This was so-called microtargeting: with big data and AI, it was possible to target individual voters based on their individual political profiles. Investigations were launched. But it was already too late: in 2016 Trump was elected. Later, the United Kingdom voted to leave the European Union (Brexit). Although it remains uncertain how big exactly the role of Cambridge Analytica was, it is plausible that there was a significant influence on these elections.

Nowadays, Cambridge Analytica is a textbook case of the political (mis)use of data analytics and AI. It shows how AI can directly influence politics, even in the broad daylight of a system that calls itself democratic. Political propaganda has always been used by politicians in democracies and authoritarian systems alike, for example, through advertisements on TV and in newspapers, but there are significant differences. With digital social media and AI, the scale and the speed are different from before; Facebook, for example, had 2,963 *billion* monthly active users in January 2023 (Kemp 2023), and communication is now personalized. Using these state-of-the-art techniques, it is now possible to swing voters and elections in a particular direction. As a former employee of Cambridge Analytica said, this means that our democracy is under threat (Le Masurier 2019). Manipulation of voters is usually considered anti-democratic. Nevertheless, it has happened in so-called democracies such as the United States and the United Kingdom. And it can happen again: social media platforms such as Facebook continue to collect data, keeping alive the potential for the kind of data analytics and manipulation by firms like Cambridge Analytica. Outside the spotlight of this particular case, political microtargeting is likely to remain in use across the political spectrum.

However, democracy is not only about voting. There are also deeper ways in which AI technology undermines democracy. "Deeper," since they have to do with the fundamentals of democracy. Voting procedures constitute only one building block of democracy; there are more elements and foundations. We need to inquire into the conditions for democracy.

Most modern political thinkers hold that democracy can only work if it is based on a number of fundamental political principles. Consider the principles of liberty, equality, and fraternity, which were seen as the basic principles of the French Revolution of 1789. It was understood by the Enlightenment thinkers of the American and French Revolutions that there can be no democracy if the state oppresses people, if people are treated radically differently, and if society is divided and knows no justice.[1] The principles of these revolutions are still key liberal and republican ones today and are the keystones of modern democracy.

Let me first review the following principles: liberty, equality, fraternity, rule of law, and tolerance. Then I will show how AI may impact these principles.

Foundational principles of democracy: liberty, equality, fraternity, rule of law, and tolerance

A first important principle is *liberty*. One of the most prominent Enlightenment figures and theorists of democracy, Jean-Jacques Rousseau, defended in *The Social Contract* (1762) the then radical view that everyone is born free. In contrast to Hobbes, Rousseau thought that the "state of nature" was not a horrible one that needs to be superseded by an authority, but a good one, which is corrupted by society. Democracy has to protect and realize the original freedom of people, rather than taking it away under the assumption that without authority, people will only fight and compete. Instead of submitting to a tyrant, Rousseau argued, people should govern themselves. If any submission is legitimate at all, it is one to the general will of the people.

This idea has been very influential, from the American Revolution to today. Where tyranny reigns, there can be no democracy. Personal liberties of citizens have been enlisted in all modern charters of rights (including human rights) and are usually mentioned first. For example, the United States Bill of Rights (the first ten amendments to the Constitution) starts with personal freedoms. Liberty is a key fundamental of any liberal democracy. Moreover, contemporary neo-republican theory (see below) stresses that liberty does not just mean non-interference and freedom of choice, but also non-domination: not being subject to arbitrary, uncontrolled power (Pettitt

1997; Skinner 2008). Even if a person's vote is not interfered with, there might be relations of dependence in which people are in a *position* to interfere in voting or have their vote interfered with. One could argue that democracy does not fit well with such relations; it requires securing the non-domination character of social relations and structures.

Interestingly, however, Rousseau also thought that *inequality* was bad for democracy. Equality of treatment can mean that everyone gets a vote and that every vote counts equally. But in his *Discourse on the Origins of Inequality* (1992 [1755]), Rousseau also argued that radical economic inequality is bad for democracy since it leads to the wealthy making laws that are in their interests, it turns the poor against each other so that they are divided and do not exercise their power against the wealthy, and makes the rich addicted to the pleasure of dominating the poor without caring about justice. More economic equality prevents this and thus supports democracy.

Furthermore, the usually neglected principle of *fraternity* requires, among other things, that the political sphere is not divided and that there is not only solidarity but also justice. As Puyol (2019) has argued, fraternity is a political principle that can be mobilized in "the struggle against the different social and political forms of exclusion, subjugation, marginalization, exploitation, discrimination, colonialism and humiliation" (2019: 2); it can be used to condemn "the social abandonment of the weakest members of society" (2019: 6).[2] In other words, a democracy that does not in some way or other care about its weakest members does not deserve the name of democracy.

In order to further support democratic inclusion, this principle can be combined with the neo-republican notion of freedom as non-domination. Developed most systematically by Philip Pettit, neo-republicanism is inspired by ancient republicanism but narrows it down to a theory of non-domination, which in turn can be framed as constituting an interpretation of what democratic self-rule means. To paraphrase Beckman and Rosenberg (2017), the idea is that everyone who could potentially be subject to domination by a public power should have the capacity to control that power. One could argue that this should especially be applied to those who are in the weakest position, that is, those who are most at risk of domination. Care and well-being are great, but justice and non-domination are better – or at least are *also* required. A slave owner might care about his slaves and even treat them well, but there is still no liberty; slavery and domination remain. In a democracy there is no place for what we may call "Enlightened slavery" – a contradiction in terms.

Other principles of democracy are rule of law, tolerance, transparency, and human rights – which in turn are related to the principles of the French and American Revolutions. For example, *rule of law* includes the key idea that the law is applied to everyone in the same way (since all citizens are equal before the law) and fairly, and that fundamental rights are respected. The state also needs to be accountable and procedures need to be transparent. The opposite of this are arbitrary decisions by an authoritarian government or the unequal treatment of citizens where the elite have more privileges. Rule of law is endangered when people are arbitrarily arrested or when a particular regime engages in forms of governance that are biased against people who are already disadvantaged. Rule of law is also a way to honor the neo-republican principle that arbitrary power and domination should be avoided: the rule of law, rather than the rule of men, is meant to secure liberty against domination (Sellers 2015).

Defended by Rousseau's rival Voltaire, and later by John Stuart Mill, the principle of *tolerance* is anchored in a particular political-epistemological view: it is based on the idea that we can be wrong about our beliefs and ideas, and that therefore we are better being tolerant. In his *Philosophical Dictionary* (1962 [1764]), Voltaire used this argument when criticizing the intolerance of the Catholic Church and in defending the freedom of the press. In *On Liberty* (1978 [1859]), Mill argued that tolerance of each other's ideas is essential for the development of knowledge since, again, our beliefs are fallible. They may not be true. Therefore, we had better allow the free expression of opinion and the subjecting of our ideas to criticism. According to Mill, truth needs to be living truth in the sense that it is discussed. Questioning and discussion is thus essential for both democracy and the development of science. Mill thought that truth will prevail if we have a free and open discussion about ideas. In the United States, this is sometimes called "the marketplace of ideas." Let ideas freely compete, and truth will emerge.

This idea of free discussion and a free marketplace of ideas is not unproblematic. In particular, there is the challenge Karl Popper (1995 [1945]) described as the "paradox of tolerance": if a society is completely tolerant, this gives freedom to the intolerant to destroy that tolerant society. Unlimited tolerance thus leads to its disappearance. Therefore, there need to be limits to tolerance (and hence to the free market of ideas). From a liberal-democratic and republican point of view, however, such limits require special and strong justification (for example, one would need to show that a particular class of speech is anti-democratic and leads to domination and potentially authoritarianism) and the limits should not be set too narrow, given the democratic importance of diversity of views, openness of discussion, and free deliberation. Current demands for more online censorship – from the left and the right – should be critically evaluated in this light (see p. 52).

Earlier, and from another angle (moral philosophy), Kant had already argued for the public use of reason. Publicity was for him a moral principle. Using your own reason requires freedom of public expression. In his famous essay "What is Enlightenment?," he argued that "the public use of one's reason must be free at all times, and this alone can bring about enlightenment among humans" (Kant 2006 [1784]: 19).

Enlightenment is about thinking for yourself, but this thinking for yourself should not be understood privately: it is a social and public activity; it needs to be done in community with others with whom we *communicate*. We can use our imagination, but ultimately we also need public dialogue; we need to talk to actual people in order to test our ideas. This concept also relates to his notion of *common sense* in *The Critique of Judgment*, later taken up by Arendt.[3] The courage Kant talks about when he argues about using your own reason is thus not only about no longer accepting being guided by authority, but also about rendering your beliefs vulnerable to discussion, about communicating and critically discussing them. Otherwise, there is only the tyranny of private opinion.

Moreover, next to these arguments about fallibility and the public use of reason, imposing one's truth on others is also wrong in terms of liberty. If there is no tolerance, some people may use violence against other people that have different beliefs. Voltaire pointed to intolerant religious authorities. But there are also many other examples of violence in the name of beliefs. In the wake of the French Revolution, for example, the revolutionaries themselves became intolerant: after the creation of the First Republic, there was the period of the so-called "Terror," with numerous public executions of those who disagreed with "the general will." Therefore, in order to avoid this and protect people's liberties, we should exercise tolerance in a democracy. The alternative is that some impose their views on others, and – keeping in mind the epistemological argument – that false beliefs flourish because they remain uncontested.

How does AI impact the exercise and flourishing of these democratic principles?

How AI undermines the foundations of democracy

AI, as it is currently used and developed, risks undermining these democratic principles in a number of ways. Let's start with *liberty*. As we have seen in the Cambridge Analytica case, AI can be used for the manipulation of people's political beliefs. Manipulation is a form of influence that is intentionally hidden – here in order to influence political beliefs. But why, exactly, is that problematic? One argument I propose is that it interferes with citizens' freedom and autonomy to form their own beliefs.[4] This is not just the usual appeal to protecting individual autonomy; instead of considering individual autonomy on its own, here the epistemic dimension of the problem is added (the manipulation of *beliefs*; see also chapter 5), and this is then linked to a conception of *democracy*. In a democracy along the lines developed so far, citizens should be free from interference from manipulation when it comes to making up their mind about who they are going to vote for. This is not the case when their autonomy to make up their mind is subverted, when their belief formation is influenced "under the radar," so to speak, that is, without their knowledge and making use of their psychological weaknesses. This has already been done using traditional political propaganda, but with AI (for example, in the Cambridge Analytica case) it is now much faster, reaches more people, and is especially more *targeted* since it is based on individual profiles, thereby fully exploiting individual vulnerabilities – the inner demons mentioned. In other words, both political propaganda's function and the resulting undermining of autonomy and democracy are far more powerful and effective.

Moreover, AI enables the automatization of surveillance, predictive policing, and judicial decisions, which translates into risks for citizens' liberty: based on these uses of AI, citizens may be unjustly arrested and detained. A by now well-known case is that of a black man in the United States who was wrongfully arrested without explanation because of a facial recognition algorithm, which misidentified him (Porter 2020). This is a problem for liberty but also for the rule of law since when such an algorithm makes decisions without human judgment and an adequate application of the law, arresting people becomes arbitrary, unjustified, and based on an untransparent process, violating the fundamental rights of people. It is also a problem for justice since using such algorithms may support discrimination against individuals and against particular groups in society (for example, in the United States context, structural discrimination against black people), which sometimes also has consequences for their rights to freedom. While the fairness of the algorithms can in principle be improved, the absence of human judgment and the non-transparency towards suspects and defendants is still problematic. Furthermore, authoritarian regimes and those who support them can use the technology to influence elections in democratic countries. And via these manipulations and threats to freedom and rule of law, AI also supports anti-democratic and authoritarian tendencies in political systems that are supposed to be democratic.

In addition, as Splichal (2022a) has shown in his work on political opinion mining, the Enlightenment ideal of the public use of reason and the free expression of opinion in the public sphere (as expressed in Kant and Mill) has been replaced by the individualization of public opinion and the technological extraction of data. Public opinion becomes a collection of private opinions. Transformed into data, it can then be used for manipulating citizens. Instead of publicly thinking, discussing, and testing ideas in community with others, and indeed instead of *constituting* and maintaining that community and public sphere through such discussion and deliberation, data science and social media merely aggregate and calculate opinions and create a situation where private opinions are mined but not tested for their "public worthiness," as Kant would have wanted it (Splichal 2022b). Together with social media, opinion mining by means of data science thus blurs the public/ private distinction and is therefore a threat to the formation of a public opinion and public discussion as the Enlightenment thinkers imagined it. It is the celebration, and often the tyranny, of private opinion.

Second, AI may be used in ways that maintain or create economic *inequalities*. Automation by means of AI often – albeit not necessarily – results in loss of jobs. And if you have a job, the algorithm might decide that you don't perform well enough or you behave in ways that the algorithm detects as fraudulent. For example, Uber manages its drivers with AI, and has been accused of unfairly dismissing drivers based on analysis of their data (HR-inform n.d.). Since this use of AI targets particular groups of workers (workers in the gig economy, who already have precarious positions) and since the decision making is automated, without human judgment, this problem can be framed as an issue concerning justice and equality, next to one of domination and exploitation. Through bias and manipulation that exploit human psychology, AI also discriminates and impacts people without its results being explainable (O'Neil 2016). For example, based on analysis of big data, people are refused credit or jobs because of their ethnic background or zip code, sometimes without explanation and often maintaining segregation, inequality, and poverty. This is a problem for equality, as much as threatening the rule of law (there is no explanation and no transparency) and the principle of fraternity (the weakest are further marginalized).

Here the concept of *justice*, in particular justice as fairness, can also be used. There is currently an emerging literature on so-called algorithmic unfairness, and fairness is a principle endorsed by many AI policy documents.[5] The idea is that since AI decisions may lead to unjust, unfair, and biased and discriminatory outcomes, such as disadvantages based on ethnicity or gender, it is important to ensure that AI is used in a just and fair way. However, empirically speaking, there are different perceptions of what is fair (Starke et al. 2022) and in political philosophy there are different views of justice and fairness, which also apply to the discussions about the ethics and politics of AI (Coeckelbergh 2022a). For example, there is a tension between universalist conceptions of justice and conceptions based on group identity: is a particular treatment by (those who use) an algorithm unfair because it does not treat everyone in the same way, or is it unfair because it fails to avoid bias against a historically disadvantaged group, for example? I already mentioned the COMPAS algorithm and the claim that it discriminates against black defendants. This claim could be justified on the basis of a universal conception of fairness – treat everyone the same, *regardless* of their personal or group identity – or by arguing that the algorithm adds to historical, structural, and ongoing discrimination against an already disadvantaged group in that particular society.

Note also that equality and justice as fairness are two different principles. Equality might be unfair in some cases and a just distribution might be an unequal one. For instance, in their discussion about the unfairness of machine learning, Mittelstadt, Wachter, and Russell (2023) argue against limiting fairness and distributive justice to a form of strict egalitarianism in which only equality of outcomes count. Bringing down everyone to the level of the worst off, for example, may well count as treating people equally, but it is not necessarily just and fair. For democracy, both principles are relevant, and the impact of AI on democracy can also be analyzed in terms of its impact on justice and fairness. (In addition, justice and fairness can also be connected to the principle of fraternity: see pp. 50–1.)

Another concept that is often used in relation to equality is *power*. As many commentators have already noted (Hawley 2021; Zuboff 2019), AI increases power asymmetries: the power of big tech threatens democracy, as does what we could call "AI capitalism." AI is not developed and used in a neutral social order but is entangled with capitalism. AI is not only a technology but also a social relation and a form of social organization. Dyer-Witheford and colleagues (2019) talk in their book *Inhuman Power* about "AI-Capital": AI is an instrument of capital leading to exploitation of human labor, control of populations, and a "concentration of wealth and social power in the hands of the corporate owners of high technology" (2019: 3). This means not only that AI contributes to general inequality in society, which as we have seen is a problem for democracy, but also that AI impacts the distribution of power: the future of AI is decided by corporate managers and their shareholders. Big tech corporations also make other tech-relevant political decisions. For example, Facebook, not democratically elected people, decides the boundaries of free speech on its widely used platform. And if big tech has such an influence on our daily lives, is it right that it is not held accountable to the public good (see also Brown 2020)? If big tech is more powerful than many countries, in what sense does the *demos*, the people, still rule? The current situation is undemocratic.

The criticism regarding inequality and power can also be made as a point about a fundamental tension between the public sphere and capitalism. Leaning on Habermas (1991) and emphasizing the Marxian dimension, Fuchs (2023) has argued that the public sphere has to do with the idea that everyone benefits from institutions, not just the privileged few, that a public sphere is a communicative system open to all (2023: 273), and that it is supposed to be autonomous from capital (2023: 277). When our communicative practices are mediated by digital platforms in a capitalist environment, however, there tends to be a "capitalist colonization of the digital public sphere" (2023: 281). Among other problems such as unequal access, undermining of solidarity, and the spread of authoritarianism and fake news, there is a fragmentation of the public sphere. AI, as it is used in and by digital platforms, can contribute to this, for example when it helps to create filter bubbles in which opinions are homogenous (2023: 282). This brings us to the next issue.

Third, AI may lead to injustice and support division in society, thus undermining *fraternity*. For example, there are concerns that AI leads to bias and polarization. I already mentioned bias and discrimination. If AI unjustly discriminates and helps to create a highly unjust society, then fraternity and thereby democracy are undermined. Another important criticism has been formulated in terms of filter bubbles (Pariser 2011) and, later, echo chambers and epistemic bubbles (Nguyen 2020). The worry about filter bubbles is that AI algorithms from platforms such as Facebook and Google present only a limited selection of information and views to users based on their preferences, and thereby offer less contact with other points of view. Epistemic bubbles and echo chambers have similar effects:

> An epistemic bubble is a social epistemic structure in which other relevant voices have been left out, perhaps accidentally. An echo chamber is a social epistemic structure from which other relevant voices have been actively excluded and discredited. Members of epistemic bubbles lack exposure to relevant information and arguments. Members of echo chambers, on the other hand, have been brought to systematically distrust all outside sources. (Nguyen 2020: abstract)

AI and social media have been said to lead to epistemic bubbles and echo chambers: people are not sufficiently exposed to other views and do not trust other sources or actively undermine other voices. This claim has been contested. For example, when it comes to the filtering of news, empirical research has shown that most people consume diverse media diets, which has led some to argue that the epistemic bubbles and echo chambers are only a problem for a minority (Arguedas et al. 2022; Fletcher 2020). Moreover, the role of traditional media should not be overlooked: television, for instance, can also lead to polarization, perhaps even more so (Hosseinmardi 2022). Nevertheless, diverse media diets do not necessarily mean that people really leave their political-epistemic bubble (they may still be mainly exposed to views similar to their own across media), and the concern about polarization and division remains relevant when and insofar as people just express their opinions and fail to really engage with others and their views – in social media environments or elsewhere. Fraternity is not only in danger when people are no longer *exposed* to other views, but also when, in the words of Gunn and Lynch (2021), people no longer treat other epistemic agents with respect and are no longer willing to learn from them. In other words, the worry is that here citizens lack the required epistemic virtues[6] for democracy and do not really communicate and try to understand each other's points of view – all very important in the republican and Enlightenment traditions.

This problem can also be formulated as a threat to *tolerance*. Combined with social media, AI may also support intolerance in the sense of discouraging listening to others and discussing ideas. Opinion wars can lead to violence and attacks on science and truth-seeking. And when AI as used in digital social media facilitates identity politics (from the right and the left), which risks dividing and polarizing, it might lead to more intolerance and a further fragmentation and destruction of communication and the public sphere. This is detrimental to democracy, according to liberal and republican traditions.

Given the above-mentioned "paradox of tolerance," this means that some limits need to be set to freedom of speech online, while keeping the public sphere as open as possible, and indeed *in order to keep it open*. AI can play a role in implementing these limits: to some extent, they can be programmed into social media algorithms. But this also creates its own challenges. Who decides the limits? Are the limits transparent?

And how much censorship – because censorship it is – is justified in a democracy?

Freedom of speech online has been widely debated. For example, Warburton (2009) has pointed to dangers, such as lack of quality control and antisocial communication: while this was possible earlier, for example, in newspapers, now millions of people can be reached at once, and much more damage can be done. At the same time, he argues, censorship is harder to implement on the internet. Today, in the era of AI, this topic is again very relevant, and I will continue this discussion in chapter 5. For now, let me note that with social media algorithms and AI (and the way they dominate what was supposed to be the public sphere), censorship is actually easier to implement, and that is dangerous for democracy. Furthermore, there is still the "paradox of tolerance" challenge. In discussing freedom of speech with regard to democracy – and when responding to widespread demands for more online censorship – we need to be guided by the normative consideration that there needs to be a balance between, on the one hand, ensuring sufficient diversity of views and, on the other hand, avoiding intolerance destroying the public sphere and democracy. As I suggested earlier, liberal democracy along republican lines must be interpreted as requiring that most of the weight be on protecting the openness and diversity of the public sphere. If not, AI risks being an instrument of censorship and will lead to the end of open society and indeed democracy.

But AI does not only risk undermining liberal democracies in these various ways; it also supports authoritarian regimes and strengthens anti-democratic and sometimes authoritarian tendencies in other regimes. As suggested earlier, the political world is more complex than can be captured by means of a simple binary opposition between democracy and authoritarian. Many political systems in the world are "mixed" systems. But this does not render the argument irrelevant – on the contrary. By supporting manipulation, surveillance, division, and intolerance, AI strengthens the authoritarian side of mixed systems and enables them to more effectively discourage free discussion of ideas and crack down on their citizens. Furthermore, systems that were already authoritarian are likely to increase that authoritarianism. Countries such as Russia and China use AI and other digital technologies for surveillance of their own citizens and for censorship, thus increasing their authoritarian power. From a liberal-democratic perspective, this is a problem for freedom, but also for other principles, such as tolerance and fraternity. Freedom is lost when the government interferes with your freedom and (for example) arrests you. But your freedom is also endangered when you have to worry all the time that you are monitored, when you mistrust the government and ultimately others, and when you therefore adapt your behavior – often in ways that amount to conforming to the rules and expectations. AI is then part of so-called "digital authoritarianism" (Shabaz 2018) in which these technologies enable authoritarian regimes to control their citizens and help to create a climate of fear, hate, and mistrust rather than freedom, tolerance, and fraternity. Ultimately, AI can be used to create a more *totalitarian* system, a form of authoritarian rule in which it is nearly impossible to escape surveillance and control by the government, and in which (as a result) citizens keep a close eye on each other and participate in state-sanctioned violence against others (who are often branded as non-citizens).

For example, Feldstein (2019b) has argued that in countries such as China, AI helps the repression of counter-groups, which without automation is usually expensive and labor intensive, by enabling control of discontent and the spread of misinformation. In a similar vein, Kendall-Taylor and colleagues (2020) have argued that autocratic governments that embrace digital technologies such as AI for surveillance have become more resilient to protests. Moreover, AI authoritarianism spreads: countries that lead in it (again, China is used as an example) often sell the technology to other countries that have similar aspirations.

Zeng (2020) has argued that it is not AI itself that is the problem but rather AI in combination with, for example, ideological components. But there is no such thing as "AI itself" anyway. AI is always linked with other human systems. Here my claim is that AI – as used by humans and integrated with other systems – does not only erode democracies but also strengthens already existing forms of authoritarianism and totalitarianism, thus violating the principles of freedom and fraternity, and rendering application of republican and Enlightenment democratic ideals, such as tolerance and the public sphere, impossible.

While there is no technological determinism, and humans and their ideologies always play a role, there even seems to be an inherent link here between authoritarianism and Platonic cybernetics, which is essentially anti-democratic. As the *Economist* describes China, using Plato's metaphor: "The [Chinese Communist] party pays no heed to dissenting individuals or unhappy minorities, any more than a helmsman (. . .) debates with passengers the safest course through a storm" (Rennie 2022). Cybernetics is not only science and technology; it is also a political philosophy, and in this form an authoritarian and potentially totalitarian one. For example, as Reijers, Orgad, and De Filippi (2022) have argued, the Chinese social credit system illustrates a move towards what they call "cybernetic citizenship": a new governance model and socio-technical system to track, evaluate, and modulate the behavior of citizens. Within the framework of such a cybernetics, AI thus risks becoming the instrument of the authoritarian and potentially totalitarian Platonic helmsman. The pilot rules and sees everything, and governance becomes a mere matter of algorithms: instructions about what to do.

In the next chapter, I say more about the origins of digital totalitarianism.

5

How AI Erodes Knowledge and Trust

Democracy is not only about procedures, rules, and principles. When we look into its conditions, it becomes clear that it also has to do with knowledge, social relations, and trust. If we want to know more about the relation between AI and democracy and better understand the risks (including the origins of digital totalitarianism), then we have to inquire into the social-epistemic basis of democracy. And today, this basis is in crisis, partly due to digital technologies. Knowledge is extended and mediated by digital media and technologies, which has given humanity gigantic new opportunities but has also led to serious epistemic problems. For example, the internet gives us information overload, there is misinformation on social media, chatbots make huge mistakes, and in a time when everyone can google, post, and create texts, the authority of scientific expertise is questioned. AI is often seen as part of the problem. Some see AI as part of elite rule and no longer trust experts – or democracy for that matter. There is a rise in populism, extreme-right movements, and conspiracy theories. AI, it seems, risks worsening this crisis rather than solving it. But what, exactly, are the potential (real) problems and what is the contribution of AI?

The problem of totalitarianism revisited:
lessons from Hannah Arendt

One way to understand some democracy-relevant epistemic problems, and how they can get worse when AI is involved, is to look again at the opposite of democracy: authoritarianism, in particular totalitarianism. While current western democracies are nowhere near totalitarianism (or authoritarianism, for that matter), studying the conditions of totalitarianism helps us to more clearly highlight the knowledge-related risks that AI poses for democracy. Totalitarianism is a form of government that does not only entail the centralization and monopolization of political power by a dictatorship (authoritarianism), but also the exercise of a high degree of control over the citizens, destroying individual freedom and interfering in all aspects of life. This also has a knowledge dimension: totalitarianism impacts knowledge in society.

To understand and evaluate totalitarianism and to study its implications for democracy and knowledge, the work of Hannah Arendt is helpful. Like many other thinkers of her generation, she argued that totalitarianism is dangerous because it takes away freedoms. Arresting people without justification, for example, is totalitarian. It amounts to the total destruction of rule of law. And in contrast to other forms of oppression, totalitarianism works with terror. She describes how totalitarianism in the form of Nazism and Stalinism oppressed the masses and exercised arbitrary power over people. Totalitarianism denies and destroys human freedom.

Arendt writes about forms of totalitarianism that arose in specific historical circumstances, which differ from those today. But her analysis can be a lens through which we can better understand the anti-democratic and potentially totalitarian risks that come with new technologies. The exercise of arbitrary power is one example of such a risk. With regard to AI, I already mentioned a Kafkaesque story of the unjustified and at first seemingly unexplainable arrest of a person on the basis of the recommendation of a facial recognition algorithm. But there is more to totalitarianism than threats to freedom. AI can also be used for the bureaucratic management of people, led and implemented by people – and perhaps in the future machines – who just follow orders. Arendt called this 'the banality of evil' (Arendt 2006 [1963]). In her report on the trial of Nazi leader Adolf Eichmann, she argued that he was not a sadistic monster but a boring bureaucrat who claimed to have just followed orders. He thus performed evil deeds without evil intentions. The problem was rather thoughtlessness, disengagement, and lack of empathy.

Now this problem can also be linked to AI and data science. Used in a bureaucratic way that alienates actual people and discourages engagement with its consequences, data science can have bad effects on individuals and society – even potentially supporting mass murder and systematic genocide – without necessarily involving evil data scientists or evil intentions on the part of these scientists. In *Privacy is Power* (2020), Carissa Véliz makes a comparison with the creation of registries of Jews by the Nazis: "data collection can kill" (2020: 114). This historical case not only illustrates the total destruction of both freedom and fraternity under totalitarian conditions, but also shows how AI may contribute to this phenomenon of the banality of evil when it is used in a social and political context that promotes thoughtless and disengaged bureaucratic use of the technology. Today, the historical circumstances are different. But it is worth keeping in mind that AI in combination with a smoothly running bureaucracy can have devastating consequences for people's lives, for example, when people lose their unemployment benefits and get into poverty because of a combination of AI-automation and bureaucratic thoughtlessness.

Yet, interestingly, Arendt also gives additional, knowledge-related reasons for why totalitarianism in particular is so morally and politically problematic, if not evil: it destroys truth and feeds on deteriorated social relations and mistrust between people. The problem is not only totalitarianism itself but also the world that makes it possible: its origins, including the epistemic world on which it feeds. First, totalitarian rules explicitly aim at the destruction of truth. Today, AI supports this aim when it contributes to misinformation and enables manipulations in elections (Helmus 2022). Here deepfakes – videos in which images of people are digitally changed so that they appear to be someone else – are especially dangerous since often people cannot detect them (Dobber et al. 2021). But the problem is not just specific cases of manipulation and lying. A larger social-epistemic danger looms over this: ultimately, these kinds of intended misinformation and deepfakes, but also non-intended misinformation such as text generated by AI that seems authoritative but contains falsehoods, can lead to an epistemic environment in which it is no longer possible to distinguish truth from untruth. And this is disastrous for democracy; worse, it is exactly what totalitarianism needs. In *The Origins of Totalitarianism* (2017 [1951]), Arendt writes that totalitarian governments create a "fictitious world through consistent lying" (2017 [1951]: 499). They disdain truth and reality, shielding themselves and their followers "from the impact of factuality" (2017 [1951]: 549). To the extent that AI contributes to this, for example by increasing the amount of misinformation and producing a kind of epistemic bubble in which factual information from the outside is rejected, it erodes democracy and ultimately contributes to creating the conditions for the rise of totalitarianism.

Second, from Arendt and the republican tradition in which she stands we can learn that democracy is only possible if we still share a world and if we are not totally isolated from one another. Totalitarian surveillance and terror by a state power work well when people are first socially disconnected, isolated, and no longer trust one another (Arendt 2017 [1951]: 628). Earlier, Durkheim (1997 [1897]) had stressed the importance of social connection and shown that its absence in modern society can lead to suicide. But social disconnection can also have political consequences: as Putnam has argued in his book *Bowling Alone* (2020), about the collapse of community in the United States, a decline in the social fabric undermines active civic engagement required in a strong democracy. With Arendt, we can add to this that it may not only weaken democracy but also create the conditions for totalitarianism. Today, it may facilitate the totalitarian use of AI for surveillance and terror by the state. Also in this sense, isolation kills.

Moreover, according to Arendt, political judgment requires *common* sense (Arendt 1968), being interested in the common good, and being able to use one's imagination to visit each other's standpoints. If we are just defending our own opinion but are not interested in understanding others' points of view, we cannot reach a common understanding. If this is no longer possible, then the basis for democracy is destroyed: not only are there no longer fraternity and tolerance, but also no common understanding and no common world. If and insofar as AI, in combination with digital social media, helps to create a political environment that leads to isolation, mistrust, and lack of interest in each other's point of view, it destroys the conditions for the emergence of common sense and thus enables anti-democratic, potentially totalitarian tendencies. True communication, in the republican and Enlightenment sense of the word, is then no longer possible. (I will say more about communication and democracy in chapter 8.)

Yet, even if AI does not lead to totalitarianism, there are more problems that are associated with AI, knowledge, and democracy.

Some challenges regarding AI, knowledge, and democracy

Looking beyond totalitarianism theory and linking back to some of the points made in the previous chapter about more general risks for democracy, I see at least the following challenges.

First, due to the kind of knowledge they produce and the ways they produce that knowledge, AI and data science can contribute to increasing power asymmetries in society, which as we have seen is problematic for democracy since it risks destroying the required equality (or at least some minimum degree of it), justice, and fraternity. AI creates an asymmetry in terms of knowledge between, on the one hand, governments and big tech companies and their experts and, on the other hand, citizens (Couldry and Meijas 2020; Zarkadakis 2020). That knowledge asymmetry is translated in a power asymmetry: the experts and the people and companies they work for gain more power. This is a problem on its own, but with regard to democracy, it threatens its fundamental principles and is especially problematic for deliberative and participative versions of democracy, which require participation of all citizens – not just experts. It is even a problem for democracy defined in terms of voting: people no longer understand what is going on in society, let alone that they can deliberate about the common good on this basis. And if you no longer know what is going on, that means others get to decide about society and its future. Knowledge is power: if others "know almost everything about us" through AI, then they have the power (Véliz 2020: 86). Citizens thus lose agency: epistemic agency and political agency. Having no access to knowledge, they do not make decisions about their data and about the use of AI. Others decide – governments and big tech.

Mining data and analyzing them with AI is great for private companies whose business model is to sell advertising based on data analysis. But they do not only sell advertising. They also collect a lot of information about us, and this information can potentially be used to manipulate and control us, for example to covertly influence what we (want to) buy. It is also tempting for governments to use AI and big data for decision making and for offering digital services. Examples of what Zarkadakis (2020) calls "automating the government" are the social welfare cases I mentioned in the first chapter, but also how governments across the world dealt with the Covid-19 pandemic. Using AI, big data, and (medical) expert knowledge, governments created an asymmetrical knowledge situation for the governance of the pandemic, which translated into a widening power gap between governments and citizens, moving societies in the direction of technocracies, perhaps even towards digital authoritarianism. Interestingly, often technocratic rule continued after the worst of the pandemic was over. As a study commissioned by the European Parliament has noted, the pandemic was used by governments to deploy a range of new surveillance measures and sometimes to replace human judgment with algorithmic decision making (Głowacka et al. 2021). This has in turn led to (more) mistrust of citizens in their governments, which have their data and make political decisions about them on the basis of these data. Right-wing anti-government movements benefit from this mistrust.

Yet the knowledge/power problem is not only due to the use and ownership of the data, but also lies in how the data are created. Datasets are sometimes not representative and exclude (groups of) people. When these datasets are then used to make decisions about people and when these decisions shape society, this becomes a political problem. AI politics thus starts with the creation of the datasets, which is a moment of exclusion. As Bartoletti has put it, we are entered into datasets by an "unseen force" (2020: 38). This also means that others make decisions about who becomes part of the dataset and who is left out. This is a political decision. In a democracy, decisions about who is "in" and who is "out" should be made democratically, that is, by the citizens or their representatives. Instead, others, in particular governments and (big) tech, make these decisions for us based on the knowledge they have. These are technocratic, not democratic, decisions.

Furthermore, we can understand these power asymmetries again as part of a particular form of capitalism (Dyer-Witheford, Mikkola Kjosen, and Steinhoff 2019; Fuchs 2023; Zuboff 2019). The current data economy is a capitalist one, which gives power to big tech. Knowledge plays a central role in the maintenance of AI capitalism. But even in a non-capitalist society in which the means of production are collective, technocracy can happen if power is centralized and based on knowledge that is not necessarily shared with all citizens. Arguably, this was the case in twentieth-century authoritarian systems that were called "communist" or "socialist." In post-communist countries such as China and Russia, we see a continuation of that political tradition, or at least its knowledge/power asymmetries. In twenty-first-century authoritarian regimes, AI helps to create and maintain power asymmetries between the centralized authoritarian and technocratic government and its citizens.

Second, in a democracy citizens need to have political knowledge and freely form their political beliefs, but it is questionable if this is possible when the use of AI contributes to manipulation, misinformation, and polarization. Even if a totalitarian form of government is not immediately in sight, democracy risks being undermined in a number of ways. Some of these risks can be formulated in terms of a lack of epistemic agency, which concerns the control citizens have over their beliefs and their formation and potential revision (Coeckelbergh 2022b). For example, if your political beliefs are manipulated, what does your freedom to vote or your right to deliberate and participate in public discussions mean? In addition, these dangers can also be conceptualized in terms of a damaged epistemic basis for the richer republican and Enlightenment ideals of democracy, for instance, deliberative democracy and related concepts, such as diversity of views, tolerance, and the marketplace of ideas. Let me elaborate this and focus on the phenomena of manipulation and epistemic bubbles.

As I argued in the previous chapter, *manipulation* is a problem for freedom and autonomy and the related ideal of democracy that requires these. By influencing people without their knowledge and going under the radar of their rational autonomous capacities, AI fails to respect them and violates the autonomy and freedom needed for democracy, which supposes that we deliberate with others and make up our own minds. But manipulation is not only a problem regarding freedom and autonomy; it is also a problem concerning political *knowledge* needed for democracy. If I am on purpose profiled by AI and then fed misinformation to influence my voting behavior, then also at an individual level the knowledge basis for democratic citizenship is destroyed since I lack sufficient epistemic agency: I am unable to sufficiently control and form my political beliefs.[1]

But there are more problems regarding the erosion of the epistemic basis needed for democracy, especially for deliberative and participatory democracy in the republican tradition. Consider *misinformation* and *fake news*. If I no longer know what is true or not, real or not, then how can I discuss with other citizens about the common good under such conditions, or even vote? Programs such as ChatGPT can produce texts full of false information. Deepfakes can offer us a speech from a politician that never took place. They can even be used to convince us that something real is false (Meikle 2022). This is very dangerous, especially in a context where trust was already eroding, such as in the United Kingdom (Meikle's example), as opposed to, say, Nordic countries, where public trust still tends to be relatively high (which is reflected in their AI strategy; see Robinson 2020). If we can no longer distinguish truth from falsehood, and if trust between citizens is destroyed, then democracy does not work.

Thus the point here is not that there is an individual right to truth,[2] but rather that *democracy* requires a particular kind of epistemic environment. The richer ideals of democracy, such as deliberative democracy, and their principles, such as the Enlightenment idea that opinions have to be exposed to discussion so that we may find out the truth together, cannot work, let alone thrive, if the use of AI leads to misinformation and fake content. Under these conditions, we cannot make a common world. This use of AI erodes and ultimately destroys the possibility of democracy – which, as Arendt argued, can lead to totalitarianism.

Furthermore, as suggested previously, *epistemic bubbles* are a problem for fraternity and are divisive for society. But they also create the wrong kind of knowledge basis for democracy since the diversity of views is reduced and relevant knowledge is excluded. For democratic voting and public deliberation, it is vital that I am exposed to a diverse pool of views and that I have sufficient political knowledge. An epistemic bubble or echo chamber decreases diversity of views, fragments the public sphere, and prevents the adequate formation of my political beliefs and views – or at least renders the revision of such views difficult. Imagine, for instance, that some people have racist views but are willing to discuss and potentially revise those views in the light of other views and scientific evidence. This requires that they are sufficiently exposed to other views and to science. But this is impossible if they remain in a racist bubble. Whether or not they are kept there on purpose (whether or not the effect is intentional), the result is the persistence of a narrow epistemic basis for the exercise of their democratic agency. In other words, they have insufficient epistemic agency for exercising their democratic citizenship.

Moreover, going again beyond the individual level, when epistemic bubbles and echo chambers encourage people to hold on to their beliefs without rendering these beliefs open to discussion, this goes against deliberative ideals of democracy and related ideals such as Mill's and republican ideas about epistemic virtue. Instead of a marketplace of ideas, we get disagreements that can no longer be bridged. There is no willingness to open up one's own views to discussion and no effort is made to understand others' points of view, if one gets exposed to them at all. Instead of a humanistic community of open discussion, we get a divided and intolerant society. Instead of Enlightenment, we get hostility towards argumentation and science. Instead of communication, we get violence.

Disagreement is not necessarily bad. It is not only unavoidable but it can even be productive, as pluralistic and agonistic versions of democracy show. Mouffe (2013) has criticized Habermasian models of deliberative democracy for their exclusive focus on consensus and has argued that disagreement and struggle can also lead to much-needed political change. The disagreements and tensions described here, however, do not seem to be productive, at least not for democracy. If they lead to social change at all, they lead to the wrong kind of social change. When, enabled by AI and related technological environments, people just express their opinions without being prepared to publicly discuss them, then violence and domination are around the corner since there is no attempt to understand the other's point of view and there is the temptation to impose one's view on others or to disregard others. Disagreement then leads to intolerance and – also keeping in mind Arendt and other republican ideas – ultimately to a destruction of common sense and of the public sphere, perhaps even totalitarianism.

While, empirically speaking, the extent to which these epistemic phenomena occur may vary (for example, epistemic bubbles may not be a problem for everyone and everywhere; they may be more urgent in some media contexts than others), this discussion provides arguments for why they are problematic with regard to democracy.

Third, insofar as AI offers opportunities for manipulation and leads to the mentioned epistemic problems, AI leads to mistrust: mistrust from citizens towards the government, but also mistrust towards one another, including mistrust of experts and scientific knowledge.

Let me start with mistrust towards the government. Democracy in its representative form is in trouble when citizens no longer have the feeling that the government can be held accountable and responds to their needs and problems. If the government uses AI and data science in ways that are not transparent (because it is hidden from public view or because the AI system used is inherently not transparent and does not offer explainability[3]), then there is a problem of accountability. Democratic governance requires that decisions can be explained and scrutinized, in parliament and beyond. Moreover, it also requires that responsibility can be ascribed. But it is not always clear who is responsible when technologies such as AI are used to automate decisions or when users try to evade responsibility by saying that it is the machine's fault. This also applies to use of AI by governments and state institutions. Imagine, for example, that your social welfare institution suddenly stops your welfare benefit by saying that the AI decided to stop it. Who is responsible for this decision, and how can we avoid nobody being held accountable? Automation of decisions can thus erode the basis for accountability and responsibility, and lead to mistrust of the government and in the end even to mistrust of the entire political system – democracy.

Note, however, that citizens' mistrust towards their government is often based on the feeling that the state does not cater for their *individual* interests. Yet what counts *politically*, according to the republican democratic tradition, is not just individual interests but the common good. We need to distinguish mistrust based on private interests from mistrust that is fully democratically justified: a lack of trust that the government takes care of the common good. The currently prevailing form of mistrust is rather a symptom of the failure of democracy and the misguided celebration of the supremacy of individual interests. Furthermore, it is not enough to point to professional politicians when it comes to solving the problem. In the republican tradition, restoring trust is not just the duty of politicians but of all citizens since governance is meant to be a matter of participation in common decisions. We are the politicians. Restoring trust, changing our political institutions in a more democratic direction, and creating and using democratically good AI (for example, AI that is transparent and explainable) is the responsibility of all of us.

But the problem of mistrust also reverberates beyond citizen–state relations. If Foucault (1980) is right that power relations also occur beyond the citizen–state nexus, then political mistrust is also an issue in relations between citizens. And these relations are also affected by AI and data science. Citizens may use AI in ways that can damage trust relations, say by categorizing and manipulating others via social media apps. But often the erosion of trust is unintended, for example, when an epistemic bubble unintentionally created by citizens increases mistrust in others outside the bubble. It could also happen that citizens' trust relations are already damaged for other reasons and that the use of AI further erodes them. All this mistrust in others and in society feeds anti-democratic tendencies, potentially leading to authoritarianism and totalitarianism, as Arendt argued. But even without leading immediately to authoritarianism, AI-supported mistrust between citizens is unlikely to foster the kind of communicative, sympathetic, respectful, and tolerant relations between citizens that are required by the richer ideals of democracy defended by Arendt, the republican tradition, and the Enlightenment thinkers.

Finally, related to the issue concerning epistemic agency is the problem that AI and data science can erode political

subjects' self-image and self-knowledge. Can we still understand ourselves as autonomous in the light of AI and other
digital technologies? This is a problem for the relevant ideals
of democracy. The Enlightenment assumption was that
we are autonomous subjects who reason with one another
about politics in the public arena. But if AI knows me better
than I know myself (or at least that is the claim of the tech
industry) because it tracks my behavior and categorizes and
influences my beliefs without my knowledge, then this kind
of political practice seems undermined. Why bother with
democratic procedures and communicative discussions if
citizens' political views and beliefs are influenced "under the
radar" of their Enlightenment reason and control – something
so important in Habermasian, Rawlsian, and Kantian
philosophical traditions? And if emotions and "voices" are
politically relevant or even important in politics, as Mouffe
and other thinkers have argued, then what happens to politics and democracy if these emotions and voices are heavily
influenced by political manipulations using AI and data
science?

To be fair, this problem is not entirely new. Modern democracy always faced the problem of social influence: when I make
up my mind as a citizen in a democracy, I am already heavily
influenced by others (intentionally or not), so what does that
say about the quality of my vote, my opinion, and my voice?
And, indeed, what does it say about the feasibility of democracy? When today that social influence is mediated by digital
technologies, including AI, dealing with this problem does not
get any easier. The point is not that things were perfect before
AI; the point is that AI makes them worse, amplifies them. Big
Brother, who already knew more about me than was good for
me, now uses AI. Or more accurately, at least in countries that
call themselves democratic: Big Other (Zuboff 2015) knows
me better through AI. Profiled and manipulated by big tech
and – in principle – anyone who can use AI applications, the

political subject that the Enlightenment wanted to establish seems far away indeed.

For sure, that Enlightenment image was also problematic and certainly not uncontested. But while postmodern and feminist thinkers have been right to criticize the image of the fully autonomous subject that denies its own relationality, and while self-knowledge is likely to change in complex ways under the influence of AI and other digital technologies (some of which may be beneficial), normatively speaking some minimum degree of epistemic agency and autonomy seems to be needed for democracy. It is therefore mandatory to create epistemic environments that produce political subjects with a degree of epistemic agency and autonomy that is sufficient and adequate for the mentioned ideals of democracy.

As noted earlier, acknowledging these dangers does not imply claiming that AI always and necessarily has these knowledge-related effects. But my arguments offer a way to frame the concerns and explain what exactly is problematic about the phenomena when it comes to *democracy*. And even if AI has these effects, there is no reason to feel hopeless and helpless with regard to AI's impact on democracy: we can do something about the problems. We can make democracy more resilient and we can make better, more democratic AI.

6

Strengthening Democracy and Democratizing AI

Given the problems indicated in the previous chapters, how can we fix them? What can we do to make democracy more resilient in the face of AI and the digital revolution? And – if we don't take AI as a given but focus on its development for good – can we make AI more democratic? How does that work?

Strengthening and creating new democratic institutions

A first step to make democracy more resilient in the light of AI has little to do with AI and more with the present weaknesses of our democratic institutions. We need to make democracy stronger. Democracy is a great idea, but it still needs to be fully realized. In particular, if we move away from the minimal, thin conception of democracy as a voting procedure and embrace a richer ideal – one inspired by republican, Enlightenment, and deliberative approaches – that includes participation, public deliberation, and social communication, then the potentially negative impact of AI and other technologies will have more chance to be mitigated. While AI is political through and through (Coeckelbergh 2022a), in itself its use is unlikely to sink democracy, unless that democracy is already seriously in trouble. If we strengthen and further develop our democratic institutions, we diminish the risks discussed so far.

One important instrument for preserving democracy is the law. As Susskind (2022) has argued in defense of what he calls "digital republicanism," the law must preserve democratic institutions and curb "the unaccountable power of those who design and control digital technology" and their market individualism, which wrongly believes that everything can be left to individuals and their companies pursuing their own interests (Susskind 2022: 11). The Constitution needs to play a role, together with universal principles such as human rights and procedures and places for settling disputes (traditionally the courts). In his discussions of AI regulation in an EU context, for example, Nemitz (2018) connects democracy to rule of law and human rights. And in liberal democracies we have parliaments, which are supposed to represent the people (rather than big tech) and who can make laws to limit the power of the tech sector. I will soon say more about AI regulation.

But beyond conservation of what we already have, we also need to build something new. We need institutional change. We need to transform our political institutions into a more participative and communicative direction. Given the current unsatisfactory performance of our existing political institutions, we do not only need to protect democracy, we also need to create it. Here recent ideas from political theory can help. For example, Landemore (2020) has proposed what she calls an "open mini-public": a jury of randomly selected citizens who deliberate and make the laws. This is not the usual idea of direct democracy; it preserves representation since it remains a selection. At the same time, ordinary citizens are involved in the decision making, rather than political elites or tech billionaires. AI could also help here (see pp. 87–91). However, it is not clear how such a model would fare, given that nowadays quite a bit of expertise is needed, especially vis-à-vis digital technologies such as AI. The element of randomness can also be criticized; is what Guerrero (2014) has called "lottocracy" acceptable? And how resistant is this model against populism and extremism? What other interventions might be (more?) productive for a knowledge-informed democracy? We need to think further about what new balances and negotiations between democracy and technocracy are needed in the twenty-first century.

With regard to the Constitution, we need to transform our constitutional order in a way that gives sufficient and effective power to democratically elected bodies as opposed to judicial powers and big tech, while ensuring that there is enough input from expertise. And if we want to realize a more republican conception of democracy, it also needs to integrate modern individual liberties with an orientation of the common good. While this raises questions about how to define the common good[1] (see chapter 8) and how to balance that normative orientation towards the common good with individual rights and liberties, such an orientation may provide a more robust normative and legal basis for our democracies, rendering them more resilient to what AI and other digital technologies might do to them. In addition, we will also need better procedures for settling conflicts between citizens, including conflicts that have to do with AI and other digital technologies.[2]

Another important democratic institution that should be mentioned in this context is quality journalism. Journalism, often called the fourth branch of government or the fourth estate, has the important task of monitoring and critically evaluating the government, next to informing and educating the public. In the light of digital technologies such as AI and related phenomena such as fake news, this is now more needed than ever. Journalists already had to fact-check and facilitate the spread of truthful information before AI took centre stage, but in the current context of misinformation promoted by the use of AI, this role becomes more important (Bimber and de Zúñiga 2020). Beyond those who play this critical role in classical media such as newspapers and TV, we need more "editors" and "moderators" of discussions in the public sphere as mediated by digital social media: we need people who can help citizens with their political-epistemic challenges. Here AI is not necessarily a threat but can assist, for example by automatically presenting articles that disrupt the homogenous newsfeed of a reader (Lin and Lewis 2022) and by playing the role of gatekeepers (Duberry 2022) in order to protect democracy against anti-democratic forms of populism and the rise of various forms of authoritarianism. As we know from the historical case of Hitler but also more recently Trump, democratically elected leaders can subsequently subvert democratic processes (Levitsky and Ziblatt 2018) and – in the case of Hitler – even establish full-blown autocracies. AI algorithms can be used to mitigate the enabling role that digital media play in giving such people a voice and contributing to their success. More generally, AI and other digital technologies can help to enhance the quality of the public sphere – keeping in mind, of course, that freedom of expression is also an important value in a democracy.

This is not to say that AI algorithms should be the only gatekeepers and editors; humans are very much needed. But *which* humans is important: fact checking and decisions about content should not be left to undemocratic actors such as CEOs and employees of Facebook or Twitter. There is a significant role for independent journalism, non-corporate editors and mediators, and publicly owned media. Governments should offer incentives and support the education and training of such editors and mediators.

Regulation and oversight

This brings us to a second and related way to deal with the challenges regarding AI and democracy, which also tries to strengthen the grip of democratic political institutions on technology development and use: regulation and oversight. If there is currently a power imbalance between big tech and democratically elected political entities, then this is not an inevitable situation or "natural" way things are. The belief in technological determinism – the view that technology shapes society according to its internal logic and thus determines our future, with only a minimal role for humans – often goes hand in hand with political conservatism and laissez-faire. As Brevini (2022) notes, faith in technology is often used as "a powerful apology for the status quo and for the current structure of capitalism, without leaving any real space for critique" (2022: 21). Moving instead beyond determinism and techno-solutionism, which wrongly believes that there is a technological solution for all our social and political problems, we can find such a space for critique and indeed for action. If there is currently a power imbalance, then we as citizens can critique, resist, and take back the power. While the private sector undoubtedly has a role to play in regulating itself and, due to its expertise and current position in the tech and media landscape, must remain a key dialogue partner and actor when it comes to policies regarding the ethics and politics of AI during the next years, the future of our societies and democracies is too important to leave entirely in the hands of privately owned, undemocratic organizations. Their position in terms of knowledge and power is neither natural nor inevitable. To take the same example as before: given their influence and success, at the moment platforms like Facebook and Twitter, and tech billionaires like Mark Zuckerberg and Elon Musk, decide what information and which opinions enter the public sphere. In a democracy, this is unacceptable.

Most of these problems are well known. We already have analyses of ethical and political challenges and opportunities of AI. A lot of work has been done, both inside and outside academia. It is increasingly recognized today by all stakeholders that we need robust policies and effective regulation that help citizens, companies, governments, and other societal actors deal with the potential risks and harness the possibilities of the technology in an ethically and politically sustainable way. This is not only important from a legal perspective, in order to ensure legal accountability (see, for example, Katyal 2022), but also from an ethical and political perspective. As I write, there are several national proposals for regulation, such as the White House's *Blueprint for an AI Bill of Rights*[3] from the Biden administration. And following the European Commission's proposal for a European Union regulatory framework on AI,[4] which is partly based on the recommendations by the Commission's High-Level Expert Group on AI, the AI Act[5] has been approved in the European Parliament. It is claimed to be "the world's first comprehensive AI law."[6] It regulates AI according to categories of risk and also proposes oversight.

Ideally, regulation and ethics go hand in hand. We should not have to choose between them. Current AI regulations and proposals for AI regulation are based on both ethical and legal principles. For example, the EU says its regulation is based on European values and fundamental rights, and the UNESCO Recommendation lists a number of values and principles, such as respect for human rights and dignity, fundamental freedoms, environmental and ecosystem flourishing, diversity and inclusiveness, no harm, fairness and non-discrimination, transparency, and accountability.[7] While discussions about AI policy have seen different views on which ethical principles should be used (for example, whether bioethics principles should be the basis, as Floridi and Cowls [2019] have proposed) and while high-level principles alone are insufficient to guarantee ethical AI (see, for example, Mittelstadt 2019), everyone agrees that ethics should be the basis of AI regulation. Note, however, that ethics is sometimes used to justify a politics of laissez-faire and self-regulation. Ethics then becomes ethics washing. But avoidance of AI legislation is undemocratic (Nemitz 2018). It leaves us with a situation in which key principles and values of democracy remain under threat and in which the rules are made by those who lack the democratic legitimacy to do so.

Moreover, it is important that the regulatory *process* is well embedded in the mentioned democratic institutions in order to avoid its being hijacked by particular interests and powers. If big tech does not avoid regulation, it does at least try to deeply influence it. Now, lobbying is also a way of bringing in expertise, and private-sector actors are some of the relevant stakeholders. But for the sake of democracy and the common good, that influence and involvement needs to be limited. Too little regulation and too much room for corporate influence on tech policies lead to the tyranny of the strongest. This is an imminent danger today when AI is often still under-regulated in many parts of the world and when big tech companies try to substantially influence AI regulation, for example in Europe and the United States.

The problem, therefore, is not just what and how much regulation we need; as the previous section proposed, we also need to critically reflect on our institutions, which apparently are hardly resilient in the face of the current developments. Democracy needs limits to power. In the light of the power of big tech, we need to revise the way power is currently distributed in society. We need new checks and balances and new institutions. For example, one could consider establishing a new institution that better links technology-development contexts to democratically elected bodies and does so in ways that redistribute power towards those elected bodies (away from big tech), while at the same time ensuring a significant role for, and communication of, expertise. One could also argue that some things should not be left to the market: that some data, some goods and services, some infrastructures, and the roles of gatekeeper or moderator are too important to leave to private initiative. One option, for example, is to turn some of the big tech companies into public utilities, as Risse (2023: 71) has proposed.

This brings us to the question of to what extent we should allow AI and other digital technologies to be entangled with capitalism. Should the technology (and its profits and benefits) be democratized, in the sense of shared or publicly owned? One reason why currently regulation does not happen or is kept minimal is the persistence of the idea that technology development should be mainly, if not exclusively, a matter of private initiative, private ownership, and private capital. But there is no reason why (the current version of?) capitalism should be taken for granted or seen as natural. As Marxian thinkers such as Dyer-Witheford, Kjosen, and Steinhoff (2019) and Fuchs show, there are alternatives. For example, Fuchs (2023) defends a socialist version of democracy, which he defines as one which "advances the common economic, political and cultural good of all humans" (2023: 13), and which would be supported by digital technologies. His socialist version of what he calls "digital democracy" (2023: 12) implies, among other things, that more support is given to independent public media (2023: 297); this would help journalists to play their democracy-supporting role mentioned earlier. In this context, it is worth noting that currently not only digital social media but also privately owned traditional media empires such as Fox News TV and the British tabloid press undermine democracy when they create more polarization and destroy trust in media and democracy.

Another way to reconsider the balance between private and public ownership of (the means for) digital technology development is to give more support to the creation and maintenance of the so-called digital commons. The idea is that digital technologies and resources such as data should be communally owned and shared. Consider, for example, Wikipedia or open-source software, which can be freely used and to which everyone can contribute.

In the critical theory literature that promotes more equality in the data economy, there are at least two different ideas about how data should be owned and distributed in a democracy. One remains within the liberal-individualist sphere and promotes empowerment of individual citizens. Fischli (2022) has argued for a so-called "data-owning democracy," a political economy in which the ownership of data (understood as capital) is distributed among citizens and in which citizens have a say in how their data are used. A different idea is digital socialism (Muldoorn 2022), which would entail common ownership of data, participation of workers and communities, and democratic control over investment – thus achieving a more radical redistribution of power that goes beyond an individualist approach.

Seen from a global perspective, the question arises as to whether one political-economic system will do. Given the diversity of systems in the world and their political contexts and political cultures, we need to connect the question concerning AI and democracy to thinking about what democracy means in relation to specific systems and contexts. There may be different versions of rendering AI more "common." Similarly, we should ask what democracy and the use of AI means in the light of ecological and climate challenges, and if capitalism and free-market thinking can sufficiently deal with these challenges. Critical theory (broadly conceived), combined with environmental theory, can help to conceive of alternative systems. But even from a market perspective, one could argue for breaking up global monopolies and oligopolies in order to preserve competition and maintain a level playing field. Antitrust laws can be an instrument for breaking up the current oligopoly of a small number of big tech companies. One could also enforce environmental regulation within a liberal framework.

Finally, given the global nature of these technological and ecological problems, regulatory efforts only make sense if there is some harmonization and coordination at *supra*national and global level. AI and its ethical and political consequences are not confined to one country or one region. Data and software cross borders easily, and so do their environmental effects. If the problem is global, we also need solutions at a global level, in addition to other levels.[8]

In the area of AI policy, recently several international organizations have taken initiatives. For example, in 2021 UNESCO member-states adopted a global agreement on the ethics of AI,[9] and the Council of Europe is working on AI policy based on human rights, the rule of law, and democracy.[10] I have also already mentioned EU policy making in this area. But the EU has a supranational aspect. It remains questionable how effective *inter*national organizations can be in this domain as opposed to what a truly supranational governance framework could do for promoting and steering democratic use and development of AI. As with many other urgent global matters, such as climate change, pandemic, and war, when it comes to global governance of AI we still find ourselves in a kind of Hobbesian state of nature: there is no global governance authority, and nationalism threatens efforts to respond to the urgent need to better coordinate. That being said, global governance has its own challenges, such as negotiating different political cultures and traditions, and of course ensuring and maintaining the democratic character of governance at such a level. For example, how to recognize diversity in approaches while still ensuring effectiveness?

The solution to the absence of global political authority should not be a Hobbesian Leviathan, that is, a global authoritarian government, but a democracy. However, it is not clear what that means at the global level. Perhaps we need a universal republic, as Cicero proposed, yet one that recognizes different levels of power. But how do we ensure that minorities and cultural diversity are protected? And how can this be realized in practice? Can existing non-democracies even be integrated in a global democratic governance structure? Should they be intervened in and forced to be more democratic, or are there other pathways? How to ensure non-domination and prevent empire and colonialism? Is a federal structure to be preferred? Much more work needs to be done on this topic; unfortunately, many political philosophers take the nation-state and its citizenship boundaries for granted when it comes to talking about technology and democracy – and indeed when it comes to defining the boundaries of the "common" in "common good" (a concept I further discuss in the following chapters).

Democratic AI

So far, I have proposed regulation and institutional change in order to ensure a democratic politics of AI. A third approach, however, crosses the divide between technology and politics. Instead of taking the technology as given, and waiting until something bad happens and then measuring the damage and trying to regulate and resolve problems afterwards, this proactive and preventive approach tackles the tech development itself to render it more ethically and politically responsible. The aim is to try to create AI that is more democratic and more totalitarianism-proof.

For this purpose, existing methods for the ethics of technology and responsible innovation can be used, but with an emphasis on politics: the reframed aim of these methods is therefore to make sure that not only ethical but also *political* values and concerns are injected into the process of tech development – including democracy. Consider, for example, "value sensitive design" (Friedman and Hendry 2019; Van Den Hoven 2013), which proposes methods to take into account human values in the design of new technologies, and the concept of "responsible research and innovation" (Owen,

Macnaghten, and Stilgoe 2012; Von Schomberg 2013), which also aims to take into account ethics by, among other things, involving stakeholders in research and innovation processes. Similarly, and entirely compatible with the spirit of these methods and visions, I propose that for the *politically* responsible development of AI, *political* values and concerns should be taken into account, and that politically relevant stakeholders be involved in its development. This proposal is also in line with the approach taken in a recent European Group on Ethics in Science and New Technologies (2023) report on democracy in the digital age, which recommends to the European Commission public participation and value-sensitive design to protect fundamental values (2023: 49).

This proactive approach implies that AI experts who are involved in policy making and decision making regarding AI have forward-looking responsibility for AI and its unintended ethical and political consequences. At the very least, this means that these experts must be informed by political and societal actors (Hedlund and Persson 2022). But better still would be political, democratic *involvement* at the level and stage of technology development.

The justification I propose is similar to existing arguments in the ethics of technology. In technology ethics, it has already been argued that technology is never neutral and has a *moral* dimension (Verbeek [2011] and earlier Latour [2002]), and that therefore we should better open and shape the process of its moral-technological development. Similarly, and in addition, one should also acknowledge, in line with Winner's (1986) and Feenberg's seminal work in philosophy of technology (e.g., Feenberg and Hannay 1995) and Latour's (2004) work on the politics of science, that technology also has an inherently *political* dimension and that therefore we should better openly and democratically shape its political-technological development. If technology is linked to political and social arrangements and to political ideologies and cultures, if its development is not only technically but also socially constructed, and if it has political consequences, then real change can only happen if we also change the technologies, not just the institutions. If power also comes from technology and not just from what people do in parliaments and other democratic institutions, then a comprehensive democratization of the AI project requires that we also modify technology. If technology is "politics pursued by other means," as Latour (1983: 168) says about science (itself a parody of von Clausewitz's famous aphorism), then we should better shape that politics and that technology. If we really care about our democracies and want to make them more resilient in the face of the challenges posed by AI and other digital technologies, then we should not only change and strengthen the political process and institutions and their democratic control over technology, but also change AI: we should make AI more democratic. Let's create totalitarianism-proof AI and *democratic AI*.

In particular, I propose *democratic AI development* (DAD) and *democracy by design*[11] aimed at supporting the growth of what we could call a *technodemocracy*: not a technocracy but a democracy that continuously and systematically reflects on, and transforms, itself and its technologies based on the awareness that technologies such as AI are always political, and that therefore aims at developing democratic technologies. We need software, innovation processes, and regulations that connect the development of technology in more direct and more effective ways with discussions about politics and democracy and, preferably, with democratic decision-making processes, democratic procedures, and democratic institutions.

While implementing this idea requires taking away some freedom from companies and other private-sector actors in society that develop AI (just as *ex post* regulation does), it at the same time includes them in the process as stakeholders and key actors from the beginning. Moreover, it also *supports* these actors since it *helps* them to develop politically responsible and democratic technology. By assisting them, it offers more certainty that they are doing the right thing and increases or maintains the ethical, political, and ultimately also the economic sustainability of their practices and business.

Note, however, that my argument for rendering AI development more "political" does not imply the claim that technology development should be *politicized* in the bad sense of the word: one that implies the *total* loss of independence on the part of the companies and one that simply replaces one centralist form of power with another. The point is not that, say, Biden should take over from Musk or Altman. But it means at least that developers and their companies must take into account democratic and more inclusive processes concerning the regulation of technology when developing AI, and ideally that the very *shaping* of the technology also involves democratic institutions and processes, even if indirectly. For example, the creation of technical standards and certification procedures that aim to make AI more ethically and politically responsible should not be left to experts alone, but needs to be linked to democratic processes and institutions. That doesn't mean that politicians who don't know anything about tech would create the standards and do the certification. Experts are needed. But democratically elected bodies and other democratic institutions need to be systematically and obligatory *involved* in the development of, and discussions about, the standards. The development of AI needs to become not so much "politicized" but rather more politically *relational*, that is, democratically and communicatively connected to the wider society.

But how does this work then? And is it enough? Keeping in mind the previous points about institutions and regulation, we must be both more ambitious and more precise. If we really want more democratic AI in the sense outlined here, we have to think about how precisely to connect, if not entangle, research and innovation processes with political institutions. Given that today much AI development takes place outside democratic control, we need to properly and rigorously embed that development *in* democracy. Instead of ad hoc deliberations about new technologies such as AI and other specific technologies (as is now the case) and instead of relying on the goodwill of big tech leaders to include stakeholder views, we need to create more permanent, institutional solutions that can mediate between politics and technology development, and between experts and citizens. For example, a new, permanent institution could enable citizens as users of AI and social media platforms to talk to experts who develop(ed) these platforms and the related AI, directly or via mediators. The results of such mediations and discussions should then regularly flow back to the development process.

While this idea needs further development, it is clear that the current situation is unacceptable from a democratic point of view; we need more effective and institutionalized bridges between the world of (democratic) politics and technology development. With Latour (2004), we can say we need ambassadors that mediate and travel between these realms. But what they do should not just be a matter of occasional help (for example, the current ad hoc committees and temporary advisory councils) or remain without any binding consequences; their role should be institutionalized and integrated in the political-legal framework. If necessary, we should change our constitutions to enable this.

Moreover, we should not take the current epistemic and political state of citizens for granted. It is true that there is a lot of ignorance, and sometimes even anti-intellectualism, as in the United States, for example.[12] Plato's complaint about the masses is far from irrelevant. But again, this situation should not be just taken as given or natural, and the problem is not totally hopeless or unavoidable. A classic republican and Enlightenment recipe for citizen empowerment is education. Democracy, especially in its richer formulations, may well *end* with rule by the people but it starts with education.

In the previous chapters, I have emphasized that democracy needs a knowledge basis. Education should help to build this basis. Dewey, for example, thought that education is vital for democracy. It is required for voting, but also for democracy as a way of life and *a way of living together*. Dewey would say that we need education for cooperation and problem-solving in society. Keeping in mind Arendt and Habermas, we could argue that it is necessary for developing common sense and communication, based on common understanding and deliberation. Professional expertise is a different matter, but one could argue that citizens need at least some basic knowledge and skills to fulfil their role in democracy. Minimally, this means that all citizens are educated about democracy and are trained in critical thinking and deliberation with others, learning the skills to listen to each other and develop a common understanding. But in the twenty-first century, it should also include acquiring some basic knowledge about *technologies* such as AI and their role in society, and developing critical and democratic-communicative skills in the context of digital social media. We need training to better understand each other (keeping in mind Arendt: to imagine the standpoint of others) and to learn to better communicate, not just in general but also and especially in the context of these media and technologies, which have become so pervasive in our lives and in our societies.

Furthermore, when it comes to higher education, those who are learning to develop AI and other digital technologies should not only be educated and trained in their discipline but should also learn about the ethical and *political* dimension of their work. In the light of the indicated problems concerning AI and democracy, we need to educate computer scientists and engineers about how AI relates to political values and concepts such as democracy. Or, better and more radical, addressing this ethical and political dimension should be *part of their discipline* and disciplining. Current initiatives regarding embedding ethics in AI education at universities in the United States (e.g., at Stanford and Harvard) and in Europe go in the right direction. In any case, it is important that such education is *integrated* in the educational processes, rather than simply added to it. Developing good software and good AI should itself include a broader notion of quality, one that is not only about functioning (immediate technical goals) but also has to do with the quality of human lives and human society, with broader democratic and societal goals, and with the common good. Democratic AI then is AI that does not only whatever it is supposed to do (for example, making recommendations on social media) but that is also instrumental in strengthening democracy and supporting the creation of common understanding and common good.

Such a democratic embedding of AI development in society thus promises to make democracy stronger and more resilient in the face of these rapid and pervasive technological changes: not by regulating existing AI or by strengthening democratic institutions (which, as I argued, are also needed) but by changing the technology and ways in which the technology is developed. The idea is that the political risks related to AI are taken into account in the development of the technology and are already discussed in education and in the various political institutions and public spaces (new and old). This would be an important improvement compared to the current situation, which is not proactive enough. And it is not only good for democracy but also renders the technology more ethically and politically sustainable, making it more robust in this sense (again, quite an improvement compared to the current situation).

However, as my remark about broader goals and the common good indicates, it is also possible to conceive of democratic AI as *fostering*, rather than merely protecting, democracy. Let me say more about this constructive approach in the following chapters.

7
AI for Democracy and a New Renaissance

My discussion about AI and democracy so far has been mainly framed in terms of dangers, risks, vulnerabilities, and resilience. But this somewhat misrepresents my project of democratic AI development. DAD is about democratic AI in the sense of making AI totalitarianism-proof, but also, more positively and constructively, about AI *for* democracy.

AI for democracy

The idea of AI for democracy is to have AI foster and strengthen, rather than erode, democracy: to develop AI as a true *communication technology* in the republican and Enlightenment sense of the word. AI should then *help* us to realize that richer, relational ideal of democracy: it should help us to build a common world, develop common sense, and work towards the common good.

AI for democracy could mean strengthening the knowledge basis of the republican and deliberative democracy ideal. For example, one could imagine a program such as ChatGPT assisting with civic education and also with deliberative processes by offering (summaries of) the required knowledge to citizens. For example, it could help to inform participants about relevant scientific knowledge, and in this way contribute to the epistemic strength of this pillar of democracy. It could also inform them about different political views, perhaps within constraints set beforehand that limit the range of views (see again Popper's "paradox of tolerance") and with some procedure in place for detecting misinformation, but generally adding to the maintenance of the diversity and plurality necessary for a healthy and rich public debate. AI could also *help* to detect misinformation and bias, rather than contribute to it.

The idea of using AI for democracy is not entirely new. Some researchers already work on technical ways to design democratic AI. For example, Koster and colleagues (2022) had an AI system optimize for human preferences and design a social mechanism that won the majority vote in their experiment. But one could also go beyond democracy as majority vote. Taking up the suggestions above, one could for instance build recommender systems that citizens can use to find information in ways that ensure diversity and quality of information and avoid bias, thus *enhancing* rather than undermining their epistemic agency and epistemic basis for democratic deliberation and participation. And there is already research that aims to enhance the explainability and interpretability of AI, which can help build the trust needed for democracy. For example, Bezzaoui, Fegert, and Weinhardt (2022) have proposed a machine-learning system that is trained to recognize misinformation and that – as explainable AI – informs users about this.

However, much of the existing research effort in AI and even AI ethics is not specifically geared towards strengthening democracy. Moreover, as Henrik Sætra, Harald Borgebund, and I have argued (2022), the current technical research that claims to do so tends to use a very watered-down meaning of democracy and lacks a connection to political philosophy and its history. There is already work that aims to connect AI ethics with AI development, both in academia and in industry; similar efforts are needed for the politics of AI, using the resources of political philosophy (Coeckelbergh 2022a) and connecting those with AI research and development. Moreover, defining what democratic AI means should not be left to experts; there is again a danger of technocracy. Instead, we need *technodemocracy*. The development of democratic AI needs to be embedded in in equitable, inclusive, and fair participation processes. As already suggested, here we can learn from responsible innovation: its methodologies can help us to assess and anticipate the impact of AI, integrate ethical and political values in AI development, and – in line with the conception of democracy embraced in this book – render AI development a more inclusive and participative process. For example, in response to threats to democracy, Bruno Frey has proposed that citizens should actively participate in decision-making processes and Jeroen van den Hoven has argued that innovation must reflect our values (Helbing et al. 2017). However, in further developing these strategies and methods, more emphasis is needed about what knowledge, experience, understanding, and communication (in the richer sense of community making and world making) are needed in those responsible innovation processes. For example, we need to figure out what the role of expertise should be and what is needed in terms of knowledge and communication skills for citizens to meaningfully and effectively participate in, and contribute to, such technodemocratic processes.

Other sources for developing AI for democracy are experiments with AI-aided direct democracy. They can help us to think about possibilities for direct democracy which did not exist previously but are now possible with AI and other digital technologies. For example, in Taiwan citizens already have possibilities for online participation and discussion (for example, they can submit online petitions and comment on the budget), and AI has been used in an online participative platform to manage the conversation (Tang 2019). Furthermore, in *Cyber Republic*, Zarkadakis (2020) has argued for a combination of machine intelligence and citizen assemblies to solve the problem of knowledge asymmetries and to save liberal democracy. The idea is to select a group of citizens whose diversity reflects that of the wider social group, which is then divided into groups, each focusing on a part of the problem. Each group interacts with a knowledge base: data repositories, human experts, and digital media. Citizens are then supposed to come up with proposals. AI can help to (partially) automate the process. For example, machine learning can select popular sentences, and in that way help the citizens to reach a consensus (2020: 67–84). AI can also facilitate knowledge discovery, help people decide if they should trust particular information, translate texts if needed, and assist with timekeeping (2020: 85–100).

This proposal exhibits a lot of trust in the capacity of citizens to govern, provided they are offered a knowledge base. This is in line with the deliberative and republic approach. It is one way to still try to implement a direct democracy model in a world that seems less suitable for it than ever. By involving some element of representation, it is perhaps less vulnerable to some classical arguments against direct democracy. However, there may be still power asymmetries within the assemblies and groups. Some have more preexisting knowledge and skills than others; this tends to influence the voice they have. For example, differences in technical knowledge or rhetoric skills will likely translate into power differences.

Note also that this is a very structured and guided approach. This is much needed. Unfortunately, we cannot entirely rely on what citizens already do with digital technology and democracy. For example, Coleman (2017) observes how citizens are engaging with one another online and proposes that we rely on such horizontal, peer-to-peer communication practices for supporting democracy. But this is not unproblematic. As Coleman acknowledges, information can be distorted.

Consider again problems such as misinformation and epistemic bubbles. Coleman's approach shows far too much trust in the democratic promises for the internet and social media made in the 1990s and early 2000s. In the meantime, we know better: these technologies and the related practices have not led to a more democratic world. And while I sympathize with grassroots organizations and civil society initiatives, I am afraid that bottom-up initiatives alone will not do. I fully acknowledge the potential. Data commons can be created, for instance (see also the next chapter). And Savaget, Chiarini, and Evans (2019) show that AI can be used by civil society to influence politics. Data can be used to audit public expenses and expose corruption. AI can also promote participation. But the case of Brazil also shows that there are powerful interests working against it, next to institutional resistances in the relevant organizations. Therefore, top-down institutional change is also needed. Today, most of us are living in larger collectives and under harsher political conditions that require urgent action to safeguard democracy. Next to supporting existing civil society initiatives and facilitating ongoing bottom-up changes, we also need political vision and leadership to initiate new institutional changes and make changes to the way the technology is developed and used.

A new Renaissance

In the light of this challenge to develop a political vision of AI for democracy, it is important to remember that AI is not just a technology but also a dream and an ideal. In order to develop a vision for AI (and indeed for democracy), we need a broader vision about the future of our societies and the planet, which can then guide the above-mentioned institutional and policy changes. For this purpose, we need not only better technologies but also better narratives and imagination. And we need people who can do this. In other words, we need to educate new generations of people who, in the light of AI's risks and possibilities, can create new stories and images of a future worth living.

This is not only about imagining a better technological future, *about* technology. We can also *use* digital technologies for creating these new stories. Here it is good to remind ourselves that the political tradition of republicanism, which inspired many of the ideas discussed in this book, has been historically connected to classical humanism as it developed in ancient times and in the Renaissance. Humanists in the Renaissance built communities of learning and talked to fellow scholars and political actors across borders. In this way, ideas spread, new political movements were born, and entire worlds changed forever. Technology played an important role in those *communications*. The media and technologies that propelled the Renaissance were books and the printing press. Today, in digital times, we need to build new communities of knowledge and communication based on digital technologies. If we want a truly democratic political revolution, we need a good epistemic basis for this. Knowledge production and communication are core drivers of democratic resilience and democratic flourishing. We need to promote and build a better-quality public sphere (indeed, create a better public, as Splichal [2022a] suggests), and strengthen trust in knowledge and society. AI and digital technologies can help with this. They can propel a new cultural and educational revolution: a new Renaissance and a new Enlightenment, based on the technologies of today (but adapted to fit their new aim) and thoroughly interdisciplinary and transdisciplinary.

Digital humanism

This "quiet revolution," as we may call it, is already on its way to some extent and in some forms. In academia, some use the banner of "digital humanism" (Werthner et al. 2022), and the idea of a new Renaissance is even gaining some traction in the business world (Recke 2017). Digital humanism[1] is a vague term, but here I take it to mean that instead of using humanism to merely *criticize* digital technologies, a constructive approach is taken: the aim is to develop technologies in line with humanistic values and aimed at the good life and indeed democracy. Another component is that the relation between humans and technologies should be studied in interdisciplinary ways. Digital humanism thus connects to normative orientations from ancient philosophy, Renaissance humanism, and the Enlightenment, but uses these ideas as inspiration for development of, and discussions about, digital technologies today. Developing and discussing AI along these lines can then be part of this digital-humanist project. One could work towards *AI humanism*.

Some of digital humanism's ideas are well known among those who already use this more constructive approach to technology and have practiced the dialogue between the humanities and the technical sciences for many decades, for example in the fields of philosophy of technology, social studies of science and technology, computer ethics, and engineering ethics. But the concept of digital humanism can be used strategically to further promote and develop this approach, especially if it is given a broader intellectual basis (a goal to which this book contributes).

The term "humanism" is of course itself not politically neutral and is used for all kinds of purposes. As said, it is often used to criticize technology, for example when in the context of discussions about AI it is mobilized to defend the human against the threat of the machine. For example, Nida-Rümelin

(2022), who together with Weidenfeld first introduced the term "digital humanism" in the German-speaking world and appeals to humanism but also to the Enlightenment, argued for strengthening and protecting human responsibility rather than delegating it to AI. However, such claims risk neglecting the more complex ways in which AI may nevertheless influence our moral and political world and tend to disregard the more positive ways in which automation through AI can contribute to society – including democracy. Often humanism has been too defensive when it comes to evaluating technology. Digital humanism can help to stimulate more constructive and proactive approaches.

Moreover, when it comes to education, the digital humanism movement also needs more support within the humanities. While today more and more computer scientists and engineers begin to understand that their technologies have ethical and societal consequences, humanities students and scholars are often still unaware of the deeply political dimension of technologies and the ways they shape our knowledge of the world and our relation to others. Here, too, a change in education is needed. Classical humanism, which focuses on discourse and neglects its media and technologies, is no longer sufficient. The library needs to be supplemented with the lab; humanities students and scholars need more interdisciplinary exchanges, spaces, and projects – indeed more interdisciplinary communications – about the politics of AI and other digital technologies.

Another barrier to the growth of digital humanism as a political-academic project is, paradoxically, the fact that it is about humans. Critical posthumanists, such as Haraway (1991) and Braidotti (2019), but also environmental philosophers and postmodern thinkers like Foucault, have criticized humanism for excluding some humans (women, slaves, native populations) and for being anthropocentric. In response to these criticisms, one could argue that any form of contemporary digital humanism needs to be sufficiently inclusive and at least consider if its approach should be extended to non-humans. All too often, digital humanism is a mere synonym for so-called "human-centric" approaches to AI and other digital technologies that are popular in the technical faculties and in policy documents. This has been helpful in promoting AI ethics. But, as said, there needs to be a broader intellectual basis, and one way to achieve this is to question digital humanism's anthropocentrism.[2]

For twenty-first-century democracy to work, then, these new forms of humanism, Renaissance, and Enlightenment need to be implemented in the education of people across the disciplinary spectrum, including both computer scientists *and* philosophers. In higher education, the required level of inter-disciplinarity for digital humanism necessitates a radical change to the structure of our universities, rather than a few cosmetic touches. This may take time. But when it can do all this, the digital humanism, new Renaissance, and new Enlightenment called for here can help us to further develop the political vision and imagination needed for creating AI for democracy and other democracy-enhancing digital technologies.

Conclusion

The challenge of this technocultural revolution is thus nothing less than to create a new social, political, and cultural order: one that is entangled with digital technologies in ways that are ethically, politically, and ecologically sustainable. It is not just about AI but entails a broader and deeper societal and intellectual transformation. In the light of the democracy ideal employed here and taking inspiration from posthumanism, this comes down to the challenge of making common sense, making community, and building a (more) common world given the current technological, political, and environmental situation. Paying close attention to technologies and how they change society and the planetary environment is key to this. If our use of current digital technologies such as AI shows tendencies that go against making a common world and leads to epistemic and political fragmentation and exclusion, we have to make our democracies more resilient and better by ensuring that education helps to create a common basis and the skills needed to act in the public sphere, *and* that our technologies are changed in such a way that they foster *communication* in the sense of sharing a world, understanding each other, and building community – potentially also at global level and going beyond the human.

With regard to human communication and community building, the point is not that we should all become the same or become one – neither at a local nor at a global level. The origin of the word "communication" is not related to "unity" but to "making common" and "sharing" (Peters 2008). When we share, we remain unique persons. And as persons we might benefit from the community and of course we retain our own interests and – keeping in mind the Enlightenment – our own individual rights. But the democratic communication twist meant here is about what we owe to the community, rather than what the community or state should do for us. In ancient Rome, *munus* meant a public service rendered by a citizen to their community; it was about public duties. Today, the challenge is how to use and change our technologies and institutions in such a way that they facilitate real sharing and public service: neither the mere defense of individual rights and interests, nor the "sharing" of individual opinions, feelings of being offended, or expressions of entitlement, but the participation in, and co-creation, of a common world. Not complaining about what the state should do for us or the making public of private feelings and opinions, but the making of the *res publica*, the public sphere, through common deliberation, cooperation, communication, and understanding. As citizens we are co-responsible for creating that common world. This will generate trust and common sense, and help to realize democracy.

For AI and the technologies that are part of its ecosystem, such as digital social media, this democratic and educational ideal means we need to make sure that they do not just enable the pursuit of private interests and the expression of individual opinions, but also foster communication and community building – not to erase difference but to encourage true sharing and building trust and understanding. Moreover, we need communities and institutions that train and cultivate communicative skills and epistemic virtues of citizens, such as being willing to listen to each other's perspective and tolerance, being prepared to render one's own view vulnerable to public discussion, and being ready to imagine and work towards the common good and a common future. All this requires not only individual but also institutional changes, for example to education, technical changes to AI and the way it is used, and changes to social media and its infrastructures. Both the public sector and the private sector have a role to play in this. If they fail to take up these tasks, the former risks becoming irrelevant and the latter anti-democratic. The future of our societies is too important to leave to technocrats or to AI developers and their companies; a democratization of AI and other digital technologies is the only way forward.

As I have argued throughout this book, this democratization of AI should be embedded within a wider effort to reform our democracies and be based on a deeper and broader discussion about that topic than is usually offered in AI ethics debates. As Himmelreich (2022) has rightly argued, current calls for democratizing AI often rely on a too narrow conception of democracy as voting and participation. Here and in the previous chapters I have shown that democracy – and how AI impacts it – is about much more than that. It is also about issues such as freedom, equality, justice, and power. It is also about the question of what kind of knowledge we need in a democracy and what the role of that knowledge should be. It is also about reflecting on our political and social institutions, about the way we organize our economies, and about education. And ultimately it is about communication and about (re) making a common world. We need changes in all these areas. If we fail to make these changes, then AI risks contributing to the further erosion and corruption of existing democracies. This would be a disaster. It would not only amount to giving up on a set of great and valuable ideals, including democracy, humanism, republicanism, and Enlightenment. It would also be a terrible loss for humanity, which risks becoming helpless in the face of the politico-technological challenges discussed and to miss out on many opportunities offered by AI. And more importantly and concretely, it would be a huge loss for us citizens as situated and vulnerable human beings, citizens who are already experiencing some of the threats and problems created by the erosion of democracy and who – in contrast to those politicians and tech oligarchs who benefit from the current situation – run the risk of having to pay the highest price for the loss of democracy: socioeconomic vulnerability and isolation. This may lead to anti-democratic responses and potentially to the horrors of authoritarianism and totalitarianism. And even if it does not, it leads to less democracy, more misery, less human flourishing, and less common good.

8

The Common Good and Communication

In closing, let me zoom in on a politico-philosophical concept that has been part of my normative toolkit during the writing of this book. At various points in the previous chapters, I have argued that AI should support the common good. I have also traced this argument back to some sources in the history of philosophy, and I have mentioned related concepts such as common sense. Let me end this book by revisiting and clarifying this normative orientation to the common good, which I take to be such an important part of the thick or rich conception of democracy I employed. I will also relate it to other "common-directed" concepts (commons, communication, community, common experience, and a common world) and further explore their implications for (the politics of) AI and democracy.

Common good and the commons

Appealing to the common good with regard to AI is not new: while not getting the attention it deserves, the concept has played a role in the discourse in AI ethics during past years.

For example, the UK's House of Lords Artificial Intelligence Committee's report (House of Lords 2018) proposed as one of the overarching principles for an AI Code that AI "should be developed for the common good and benefit of humanity" (2018: 125). And in a Carnegie Council opinion piece Kaspersen and Wallach (2023) ask: "How can we ensure that the technologies currently being developed are used for the common good, rather than for the benefit of a select few?" As is clear from my comments throughout this book, I could not agree more with this.

But what does the common good mean? When the term is mentioned in AI ethics and policy documents, it is usually not defined (Berendt 2019). Often it simply means that everyone should benefit from AI, not just the few. I endorse that view, but there are more meanings and there is much more to say about it. In political philosophy, the term is somewhat controversial: as I explained, it is rooted in a particular theory (or cluster of theories), and not everyone thinks it should be a central political goal. In order to clarify what *I* mean by the term, and to further develop and wrap up this part of my argument, let me (re)visit the discussion about common good in political philosophy and show what is at stake for the discussion about AI and democracy.

In the previous chapters, I already mentioned that the term "common good" plays a role in traditional republican theories of democracy, for example in Aristotle, Rousseau, Tocqueville, Dewey, and Arendt, but also in more recent deliberative, participative, epistemic, and neo-republican democracy theories. Let me further unpack the concept.

In the Aristotelian tradition, the common good is not the aggregation of individual good or, as in utilitarianism, the greatest amount of pleasure or preference satisfaction for the greatest number of people. Instead, the idea is that (democratic) politics should not only, and not primarily, be about the fostering of private interest and individual good but about what is shared and beneficial to all members of a given political community. It should be directed to the flourishing of the *polis*. I have already pointed out that the citizens of the *polis* benefit from the common good but are also supposed to contribute to it. As Hussain (2018) puts it, they have a "relational obligation" to care for the common good. The emphasis is on the public and common dimension to politics and to democracy. Aristotle even argued in *Politics* (1998) that the good of the city-state should take priority. In political decision making and in their public life, citizens are supposed to transcend their private interests and concern themselves with the common good. This does not only promote the common good (and, according to Aristotle, virtue and the good life) but also avoids corrupt politicians and corrupt governments. Ultimately, it protects against tyranny.

This idea of the common good has been very influential in the history of political philosophy. For example, Thomas Aquinas, standing within the Aristotelian tradition, argued that the law should have the common good as its object. This influenced Renaissance thinking (e.g., Machiavelli) and later the concept can be found in the work of Rousseau, Smith, Marx, Mill, Keynes, Rawls, and many other thinkers. It also influenced modern politics. James Madison, one of the United States' Founding Fathers who had a key role in drafting its constitution, urged his fellow citizens to cooperate for the common good and saw the unequal distribution of property as a key factor that divides society. The *Federalist Papers* argue for rulers who have the wisdom to discern and pursue the common good.[1]

In contemporary political philosophy, the notion of the common good plays a role in the already-mentioned neo-republicanist democracy theory. Pettit (2004) has argued that the goal of democracy is to promote the public interest and serve the common good. He links this notion to his central concept: non-domination. In a republican democracy, Pettit argues, the state is justified to interfere with people for the common good, but not in a dominating way (2004: 150) or in a way that is arbitrary. The principle of freedom, one of the pillars of democracy, is thus interpreted in terms of non-domination and this limits for Pettit how the common good can be supported. That limit helps to keep the democracy liberal. This is an important challenge in modern politics: in a liberal democracy, working towards the common good needs to be balanced with the principle of (individual) freedom.

But what is the content of the common good (or the public interest, for that matter)? Contemporary political theorists have disagreed about whether the term can and should be defined in a substantive way without further justification – with democracy then trying to realize this so-called "regulative ideal" – or if it should be seen as the outcome of participative and deliberative democratic procedures. Such procedures are then supposed to track the common good: good which is not defined beforehand but needs to be figured out in and through a deliberative process. In Dewey's view, it is a matter of trial and error, experiment; there is no a priori conception of the common good. It is also a matter of real deliberation; the focus is not so much on ideals.[2] This solves the problem that not only we often disagree about what democracy means but also that we may not even *know what we want* when we say that we want democracy. Dewey's answer is: let's find out together.

Indeed, a main objection to substantive theories is that they disregard that we may disagree about what the common good is. One could respond that this is mainly a theoretical worry and that in practice there is often agreement. For example, in the case of AI, many people seem to agree that it is problematic when AI leads to a highly unequal and unjust society, with power concentrated in the hands of big tech and benefiting the few rather than the many, and that this does not promote the common good. Similarly, today there is a growing consensus that part of what "common good" means is having a sustainable economy and a clean, non-polluted natural environment. The problem then is not so much about knowing or defining the common good but rather that some of us do not share this aim and do not support working towards it because it is not in their immediate interest to do so. In other words, many people may agree what the common good is and what it means, but nevertheless follow their private interests. In the best case, they think that others should solve the problem: this is so-called free riding. In the worst case, however, they don't care about the common good (even if they might know what is meant by it), or they may even try to mislead others into thinking that what they do contributes to the common good. As Marx and Engels argued in *The German Ideology* (2014 [1864]), typically the ruling class tries to present its interests as the common good. From another angle, Pettit (2004) also recognizes that a system might misrepresent certain private interests as public interests (2004: 166). And there is the danger that one person or group of persons tries to impose their version of the common good on others, for example, when in an authoritarian system rulers use utopian narratives and collectivist propaganda for this purpose.

Yet even in a well-functioning democracy there is bound to be disagreement not only about what the common good is and about what balance there should be between common good and individual interests and rights, but also about what supporting the common good then means in practice. For example, even if most of us agree about sustainability as a goal, that does not mean that we would all agree about how to reach that goal and how pursuing that goal should be balanced with private interests. Does in this case regard for the common good mean, for example, that we should stop driving cars or stop eating meat? Should this be mandatory, coerced? Some people might not be prepared to give up their liberty – a value which, as I have argued, is also foundational for democracy, and which is related to Pettit's notion of non-domination. In any case, one needs to recognize that there are different interests, for example, not only the interests of the collective at large but also individual and group interests. One also needs to account for some degree of pluralism when it comes to political values and principles. There are many values, and even if we agreed on some values (which is not straightforward in a multicultural world), then we might disagree on which value should be prioritized in a particular case and what realizing that value means in a particular context. This renders using the term "common good" in a substantive way problematic.

In the light of these challenges, procedural approaches are attractive since they seem more compatible with a pluralistic view of society and democracy. If we disagree about what the common good means and implies in practice (but still agree that we should promote it), let's talk about that and find out together what it means in practice, here, and for us: let's discuss and deliberate what is good for our political community. In Kantian, Habermasian, and Rawlsian views, this is about public deliberation and use of public reason (although such accounts are not purely proceduralist).[3] The idea is to deliberate and find common reason(s) that can be shared by citizens with different backgrounds within a pluralistic society. In Dewey's view, however, the procedural approach becomes more experimental: let's try out what works for us, let's experiment. Dewey rejected foundationalist approaches (and an appeal to abstract reason) and proposed applying experimental methods to democracy. Democracy is then about common learning and growth, learning and growth at the level of the collective – not just at the individual level. In republican relational thinking, both levels are connected. Moreover, in order to make sure that different interests and values are included, one could make the deliberative and participative process more inclusive. This relates to the question of *who* is invited to the table – a power question. And with a nod to Mouffe (2013), one could and should allow for the opportunity to contest a particular definition of the common good. If this is not possible, then the danger of authoritarianism is again around the corner.

However, these approaches do not entirely exclude each other. While from a deliberative-experimental perspective (say, a Deweyan perspective), one would have to reject a foundationalist approach to the common good, one could still agree to work towards the common good based on a broad consensus on what that means even before deliberation. One could thus include substantive elements as starting points and constraints to the discussion, and use the deliberative process for discussing how to reach the overall goal (the common good) and for balancing different values and interests. It has also been argued that substantive elements may be needed since a procedure alone does not *guarantee* the realization of the common good (Blum 2016), although this begs again the question what *can*. A proceduralist and experimental approach overall avoids this problem, and a Deweyan version can live with the fact that there are no guarantees. Democracy needs foundations (in this book I have listed a number of principles and knowledge requirements) but not *that* kind of foundation: within a Deweyan outlook, there is no such foundation or guarantee.

For AI, this means that we need AI policy making that explicitly aims at the common good and deliberative technology policy making to find out what the common good means and implies in the context of the use and development of this technology and in the light of current societal challenges. This entails the development of public deliberation about AI and the common good, but also experimenting with the technological development: finding out what AI for the common good means by trying out different versions of AI. Perhaps even AI legislation(s) should be seen as an experiment, especially in the light of rapid technological changes (consider how fast large language models developed) and the uncertain impact of the regulations. Let's think about ways to make the regulatory process both faster (for example, the EU's AI Act has been years in the making, and in the meantime a lot has changed) and more flexible.

Yet this is not only about politics *about* AI; as already mentioned, AI can also *help* and perhaps even *improve* deliberative processes and help to monitor and study the sometimes daunting but also exciting and potentially highly beneficial socio-technological experiment that AI and digital tech have become. There is a sense in which we are already living the experiment. As many of us use AI-based search engines and text generators, for example, we are living the AI experiment and we all participate. However, unfortunately we do so without having given our individual or collective consent, and it is done in a non-democratic way, led by big tech. The challenge is to conduct this socio-technological experiment in a more democratic way than is the case today and in a way that is directed towards the common good.

Note that this discussion about the common good and democracy can also be framed again as a problem concerning knowledge and democracy. I have already argued that knowledge is needed for democracy. But what kind of knowledge, and knowledge for whom? With regard to the common good, one can go in a more Platonic direction, as epistocracy theory does, and put emphasis on the need for expertise and knowledge of the common good, which requires the involvement of experts who as Platonic Guardians somehow know the common good and know how to reach it. Or one can emphasize the participative dimension of procedural solutions and argue that whatever the common good is (and whatever experts and philosophers say about it), what matters if we want *democracy* is that we need a legitimate democratic deliberative and participative procedure to define what it means for us and how it can and should be attained, in this time and in this society and *polis*.

Luckily, these directions are not necessarily mutually exclusive. Throughout the book, I have suggested that we need both dimensions. In modern society, we need experts; their

expertise needs to flow into the deliberative processes, especially when it comes to answers to the question of *how* to reach
the common good. Technologies such as AI can help with this.
But we should avoid a technocracy if that means a system in
which *only* experts rule, helped by science and technology: a
system in which they claim to know what the common good
is (as opposed to the ignorant citizens) and then impose their
definition onto society. At the same time, we should avoid a
system in which experts are no longer welcome and no longer
trusted at all; this, too, destroys democracy in the richer sense
endorsed in this book.

Finally, when one defines the common good in contrast to
private interests, then one could, more positively, argue that
one should aim at the protection of, and the making of, what
is literally in common: common *goods* (plural). This leads us to
the concept of the *commons*.

The term "commons" refers to resources that are shared and
available to all members of a particular society or community –
resources that are "free" in that sense. Often natural resources
such as air and water are seen as commons, although even they
are sometimes privatized and monetized. Cultural goods such
as art and architecture are also often defined to be part of the
commons. Consider for example the UNESCO World Heritage
program: some historical sites, buildings, and towns are seen
as part of the heritage of humanity. One could also discuss
whether means of production, agricultural lands, information,
and technologies should be part of the commons. I already
mentioned the idea of digital commons. The internet can also
be seen as commons (Lessig 2001); in the 1990s, the internet
was often associated with freedom (Barker 2015). And isn't the
earth as a whole a (global) commons, a *free* earth?[4]

One way to protect commons is to make them property
of the state: to render what the Romans called the *res com-
munis* part of the *res publica*. But public ownership is not
necessary for a good to be considered part of the commons.

For example, air might well be regulated in particular contexts (e.g., in response to air pollution) but is not itself owned by the government. And Wikipedia, for instance, can be seen as part of the digital commons but is not owned by a (particular) state. But why do commons need protection in the first place? A well-known concept in political philosophy and economics is the so-called "tragedy of the commons"[5]: when individual users of the commons just follow their self-interest, this leads to a depletion of (finite) common resource(s). The degradation of the natural environment is often seen in these terms. Is this also a problem for digital commons, or do they not have this problem of depletion? Dulong de Rosnay and Stalder (2020) have argued that while data and information are not affected by overuse or exclusivity, there can still be various forms of degrading and pollution (think again about misinformation, for example), and instead of sharing and self-governance there tends to be lack of participation, underrepresentation of certain groups, appropriation, and surveillance capitalism.

For AI, creating and taking care of the common good understood in terms of commons could imply the creation and maintenance of data commons and the partial or complete de-privatization of technologies and infrastructures required for AI. The idea is then that AI (e.g., large language models or search algorithms) and the data it uses should be accessible to all and should benefit all – an idea that still inspires some tech people in the AI world.[6] Moreover, the various forms of degrading and appropriation should be avoided. These goals could be reached through regulation, if necessary public ownership, of AI, data, and the required digital infrastructures. There are also already data commons initiatives.[7] Mazzucato (2018) has argued that data should be made into a public good, allowing citizens rather than tech giants to shape the digital economy.

To conclude, in this book I endorse a version of democracy that is directed at the common good (perhaps also including the creation, maintenance, and curation of commons) and that has deliberative and experimental procedures to track and create that common good. The latter is important since it may not entirely be known beforehand what the common good is since there are different views of the common good and different interests and values connected to the discussion, and since in a democracy we need to avoid one actor (e.g., a tech company and its owner) imposing their idea of what the common good is. Therefore, it is both desirable and necessary to deliberate and to experiment: we need to involve citizens in the project of AI for common good, and we need to use trial and error at least to some extent. AI, then, needs to be developed and used within such a democratic framework and should help to support, rather than undermine it. And if in a sense AI is already a large-scale socio-technological experiment, we need to render that experiment more democratic.

The common good thus defined is then not only a guide for the good and democratic use and development of AI; it is itself also partly the *outcome* of the development of AI *for* democracy. Moreover, AI and other digital technologies can play a role in this process towards (more) common good. They can and should help to create common good, common knowledge, and common experience, and they can and should assist deliberative and experimental processes of finding out the common good together. Fostering the common good can also mean protecting and creating commons, for example, language models commons and data commons.

Finally, when it comes to setting the boundaries of the collective that makes the decisions, we need to make sure that the mentioned democratic processes of voting, deliberation, and experimentation are sufficiently inclusive. The democratic processes should also take place at various levels: within local communities and nation-states but preferably also at the global level. Given the global reach of AI and related technologies, some form of global governance seems necessary.

We then also need procedures for dealing with potential tensions between the common good of different collectives, for example, between the common good of local communities and the common good defined in the context of a nation-state or humanity. (However, I will not further discuss this issue here.)

Communication and community

Other relevant "common-directed" concepts already mentioned earlier in this book are communication and community. They are linked to the relational conception of democracy defended by republican thinkers. But what do they mean, and what do they imply for the project of AI for the common good?

Usually, communication is defined in a technical way: it is understood in terms of sending and receiving information, exchanging information. This notion is dominant in the discussions about "information and communication technologies," and in cybernetics it is linked to control and (self-)regulation. However, as I have already suggested, there is also another meaning of communication, one which can be summarized as "creating the communal" or "creating community." Instead of focusing on the quantity of communication, which digital technologies obviously deliver and which in principle can contribute to the knowledge basis of democracy, we should consider the quality of the communication, with quality evaluated in terms of the contribution to community making and to the common good. From a republican point of view, creating communicative relations between citizens is itself important; communication is then about people and not so much about information and control. And, as I noted earlier, with Arendt we can add that it is important in democratic political communication to try to understand others' points of view and to make common sense. This offers a more relational view of both communication and democracy.

From a liberal-democratic perspective, however, mentioning the term "community" gets us into a politico-philosophical minefield that in contemporary political philosophy emerged since the 1980s, when so-called communitarians challenged classical liberalism by shifting the emphasis to community. Appealing to community raises many questions. What should the role of community be in a liberal-democratic society, if such a system is sustainable at all? What should be the relation or balance between the individual and the collective, the person and the community? Does an emphasis on community necessarily lead to traditional or authoritarian systems? What can and should the role of community be in modernity?

Like Aristotle, communitarians such as MacIntyre, Sandel, and Taylor argued that community is primary and the individual secondary. Charles Taylor (1985), for example, argued that a liberal society can only work if citizens have a sense of community based on their shared conception of the common good. According to him, this means that citizens need to have some common form of life that is seen as "a supremely important good" (1985: 213). But does this way of thinking lead to embracing a form of collectivism, perhaps the kind of collectivism that we see in some authoritarian or totalitarian regimes? What are the rights and liberties of individuals within a communitarian political order? Liberals are rightly worried about this. But with Taylor and others, one should equally question how sustainable liberal democracy is *without* any role for community, given that we are social and relations beings. In the *Politics*, Aristotle famously writes about "political animals": we are the kind of beings that (need to) do things together and (need to) live in communities. According to him, this matters for politics. In this view, politics is not about individuals but about the good of the *polis* and about what we have in common. We need the *polis* and the *polis* needs us; we are political beings in this sense.

Seen in the light of history, and taking into account non-western worldviews, this way of thinking is standard rather than the exception – if anything, it is the western form of individualism that is exceptional. Many other cultures and civilizations also have and had relational ways of thinking about human beings and politics. This is an attractive direction but also poses some challenges for liberal democracies. One the one hand, there is much wisdom in this relational way of thinking about humans and about living together, and it seems to me that a democracy that neglects the basic social and political relationality of humans is not viable. On the other hand, it is important to integrate these notions of community and relationality in modern political thinking in ways that at the same time respect liberty and individual rights. This also raises the important and challenging question of how individual rights and the common good are and should be connected. For example, with Pettit we could argue that striving for the common good should be constrained by the principle of freedom and non-domination. However, this does not solve the question of how important individual freedoms and rights should be vis-à-vis the common good. Perhaps this question itself cannot be fully answered by philosopher-kings but should be submitted to democratic deliberation in particular situations, given that specific answers and balances may differ between different political-cultural contexts and when confronted with different collective problems.

This is not the place to engage in an extensive discussion about liberalism versus communitarianism (nor about relational thinking, for that matter). However, let me note that the republican tradition I have been drawing on in this book clearly has a community dimension to it. The common good is good for *us*, that is, for a given political community. One may discuss the nature and border of this community, ask how substantial that community needs to be, and question how an emphasis on community is compatible with liberty, but at the very least it should be acknowledged that according to this republican direction of thinking, community is not necessarily anti-democratic. Rather, the republican idea is that politics and democracy are at the least *also* a matter of political community. And it seems to me that that community needs to share *some* values and goals in order to work as a political community and indeed as a democracy, though perhaps not necessarily all values and goals – this brings up again the problem of pluralism and diversity. In any case, in such a democracy and in a modern pluralist context, the common good can function as an overall goal and normative orientation that organizes the community and facilitates and constrains cooperation, deliberation, and democratic experimentation.

If I claim that AI should promote the common good, then, this implies defending some degree of community (making), at least as a goal or ideal. However, in contrast to traditional and conservative versions of community, here community is not meant to work in opposition to modern Enlightenment principles such as individual liberty and rights but is instead meant to be compatible or even be integrated with it – however challenging this project may be. Furthermore, the community meant here is not fully given (even if there are traditions), not fully available beforehand, and not tied to a fixed identity. It is partly given but also needs to be made, and while it is in the making (and perhaps it is always in the making, it is an ongoing process), it functions at the same time as a regulative ideal, together with the notion of common good. But community and common good are never just abstract ideals; they are embodied in the practices, in the forms of cooperation, and in the forms of life. Yet they are not only a starting point but also an outcome. They are also a matter of trying out things and improvising, faced with particular problems and situations. They have an open and experimental dimension.

Thus, like AI, the democratic republican community itself is an experiment. It is not known beforehand how such a community might look. And there remain serious challenges. For example, it is a challenge to bring together common good and individual rights, and it is a challenge to connect to traditional notions of community while at the same time engaging in *making democracy* in response to the present situation (one which is very much shaped by technology). There are traditional elements (e.g., traditional wisdom and traditional ways of doing things), but in modern society the experiment is not limited to these elements and not constrained by them. In the democracy I have in mind, the community and communication must be open and allow for plurality.

Seen from this perspective, AI then needs to be a "communication technology" not only in the sense of dealing with data and giving us information about patterns in these data but also in the sense of working towards the common good and helping to create (more) community as part of making democracy. What this means in practice is not clear beforehand and in the abstract, but needs to be *done* and experimented with in particular contexts and in response to specific societal problems.

One factor that is important in creating such a community and democracy is common knowledge and common experience. AI and digital technologies can help us with the creation of such an *epistemic and experiential commons*; by contributing to common knowledge and experience, they can help to bring us together. This should always be in the form of assistance rather than replacement since human wisdom is also needed, that is, knowledge rooted in human embodied, relational, and communal experiences as situated political animals. If well integrated in the relevant epistemic and communicative processes, however, AI and digital technologies can in principle complement or help us to build that knowledge and experiential basis. They can play a role in *communicating* in this sense, in community making and working towards the common good.

However, currently AI and digital technologies – as embedded in specific forms of power distribution such as laissez-faire capitalism and the quasi-authoritarianism of big tech – seem to rather support a system that aims at the good of some individuals (some tech investors, tech owners, and their companies) instead of the common good, and that privatizes both the resources and benefits of what arguably should be common, shared, and *communicated*. Instead of creating more community and enriching the commons, the technologies seem to divide people and result in less trust, less sharing, and less common good. This is not to say that there is no common good or communication happening at all, but the current system enables only common good and public sphere to some extent. It also tends to be about the good of a rather small community of billionaire owners of tech companies (and some of their employees and transhumanist prophets). What is common good in the context of AI and digital technologies is now defined by people like Elon Musk, Sam Altman, and Mark Zuckerberg, rather than democratically, and often barely hides the mere and ruthless pursuit of private interests. The category of those who benefit from AI is also socioeconomically, culturally, and geographically limited. We need more common knowledge and experience that crosses these divides, and we need to use and develop AI in ways that contribute to the common good and to community making in many places and contexts. This requires regulation of AI and data in ways that render them more common as opposed to private and, more broadly, a policy of technology and indeed of economy that significantly and boldly reorganizes how technology is developed and used in society in ways that are directed to common good and community. Such a substantial change requires political leadership and democratic policy making in institutions at national and international level, but bottom-up initiatives also need more support. Ideas such as platform cooperativism (Scholz 2017), for example, which entails that workers, rather than capitalists, own digital platforms, can be an interesting and useful intervention in the current form of capitalism.

To conclude, I see communication not only as a technical procedure or as part of a (political) cybernetics but as the making of common good and community. Liberalism needs to be at least supplemented with, if not transformed by, some recognition of the relationality and communality implied in the political and the human beings on which it relies, while maintaining (other) important democratic values such as pluralism, liberty, and tolerance. It should ask us to strive for realizing and making the common good while recognizing that we can (and should be allowed to) disagree about some things, and while maintaining freedom and non-domination, one of the principles on which liberal democracy is built. AI, then, needs to be a fully democratic communication technology also in this sense: one which contributes to the building of community and is guided by wisdom and experience – including traditional wisdom that is part of the existing community and form of life – while respecting basic liberal-democratic principles such as freedom and non-domination. AI can and should assist communication in the sense of community making and should be directed at the common good, but that communication (understood in this deeper sense) must be subject to normative and epistemic constraints: it should be guided by basic liberal-democratic principles and the epistemic environment should be regulated in ways that support the common (rather than divide), maintain diversity and pluralism, encourage experiment and openness, and avoid anti-democratic tendencies. If AI and digital technologies are used and governed in this way, leading to new common experiences and creating common good, they are not tools of control (as in authoritarian cybernetics) but technologies of *communication*.

Common experience and building a common world

Finally, this understanding of communication is how I interpret
Hannah Arendt's claim that we have to create and maintain
a common world. Arendt argued in *The Human Condition*
(1998 [1958]) that the experience of sharing a common world
with others helps us to develop a common sense. "World" thus
refers here not only to a collection of things (though Arendt
also recognized that human artifacts can gather us, for example, a table) but also to common experience – the sharing
of a "world" in the phenomenological sense of the word, as
can be found, for example, in the works of Heidegger and
Merleau-Ponty. This sharing of experience is politically and
democratically significant. Combining Arendt's concept of
common world sharing with what I said about communication, one could say that communication in the specific sense
I propose here is the making of a common world through the
making of *experiential commons*: experiential meeting grounds
where different perspectives and experiences come together
and where one's own perspective and subjective experience are
not only imaginatively (Kant, Arendt to some extent) but also
communicatively transcended.

The point is that just as it is impossible to have a resilient
form of democracy without working towards the goal of the
common good (and figuring out together what it is and how it
can be reached) and without having *some* degree of community, it is impossible to have a sustainable democratic system
without (making) a common world: without creating, sharing,
and using common knowledge and experience, and without
transcending one's own perspective and experience.

With regard to AI and digital technologies, this means that
we should use and develop the technologies and media in
such a way that they do not lead to a situation in which we
each have our own world (or where each group has their own
world), and in which we have difficulty in transcending our

own perspective. We should make sure they help to create a common world.

This is especially important in the light of the political-epistemic risks related to AI. I already mentioned the problem that the use of AI can lead to misinformation and polarization. This epistemic disintegration creates a lack of trust but also social and political divisions; it leads to the political loneliness that Arendt warned about, the absence of community, and being locked into one's own experience. Democracy needs common experience and a common world. And since, like community, such a common world is never just something given, and certainly not given in the modern world, democracy as *doing* democracy is about *creating* that common world. AI should help us to make that common world, rather than dividing it or hindering its creation.

Do we have a viable alternative? One may reject the ideal of democracy articulated here and consider using AI in combination with a thin form of democracy (majority voting and indeed our current "democracy"). One could also imagine an AI that uses a utilitarian notion of the common good to govern us; this guardianship would mean the end of democracy. If we care about sustaining and creating a better and richer kind of democracy, however, one that is less vulnerable to anti-democratic forms of populism and does not lead to totalitarian nightmares, we can and must do better: we can and must imagine and develop AI as a *communication* technology, understood in the richer, *political* and democratic sense of communication developed here.

I worry, however, that as things stand, we are doing quite the opposite. If the republican philosophical tradition is right about what conditions are needed for democracy, then I fear that with AI as it is currently used and developed, we are undermining democracy. Ultimately, this may lead to creating the conditions for totalitarianism: a political system that is only or mainly about control and that originates in a world in which people have no longer something in common, are not prepared to consider others' perspectives, are no longer willing to work towards the common good, and no longer *communicate*. The loss of this communication and the need for (re)building a common world was Arendt's concern after World War II and after the horrors of Nazism and Stalinism. Today, in the current political predicament and in the light of the possibilities and dangers created by AI, it should be our concern too.

Executive Summary for Policy Makers

Given that current uses of AI are often linked to manipulation and authoritarian power, is AI good for democracy? AI as it is currently developed and used risks undermining the fundamental principles and knowledge basis on which our democracies are built and does not contribute to the common good. But if we embrace a richer, more republican notion of democracy and better understand the broader political dimension of technology, the following pathways towards more democratic AI open up:

1 Regulate, but also and more fundamentally readjust, the *power* balance between private corporations and democratic institutions and embed political values and principles in *technology development and innovation processes*. For example, have parliaments rather than private companies decide what ethical boundaries should be set for automated text generation and chatbots, bring more AI technologies and data into the commons, and make it a legal requirement (next to incentives such as certification) that companies assess the ethical and political impact of their new AI technologies before they are released.

2   Strengthen existing democratic institutions to safeguard fundamental democratic principles and rights, but also create *new institutions* that are more deliberative and participative, facilitate and guide socio-technological experimentation, are supported by AI and digital technologies, and enable mediation between expertise and democratic decision making in a more permanent, systematic, proactive, and faster way. For example, use AI-assisted mini-publics to deliberate about the use of AI and set up a permanent council made up of both experts and lay people that offers recommendations to the government regarding AI and other new and emerging digital technologies and that is able to respond fast to new technological developments. Create fast-track law-making procedures for more responsive and potentially experimental tech regulation that can be more easily adjusted.

3   Invest in education and facilitate new communities of interdisciplinary and democratic learning. We need not only technological and institutional changes but also changes in education and culture, perhaps a new digital humanism and a new Renaissance and Enlightenment. For example, support bottom-up discussion initiatives and hacking for democracy, integrate interdisciplinary education at all levels and in both technical disciplines and the humanities and social sciences, and invest in academic research and facilitate public discussions aimed at rethinking humanism in the light of AI and digital technologies.

4   Aim at the common good and strengthen the conditions for democracy by not only focusing on control but also and especially on facilitating communication, understood as making community and building a common world. Consider, for example, the creation of long-term tech policies aimed at the common good, cooperativist technology development, technical measures that work against epistemic bubbles, polarization, mistrust and hate, and

education that does not only transfer scientific knowledge and language competences but also develops critical skills vis-à-vis digital technologies such as AI and trains people to see each other's view and discuss the technological future and indeed any other matter in a respectful and constructive way – thus supporting not only democracy but also ultimately helping them to better live together.

Notes

Preface

1 See, for example, https://www.bbc.com/news/uk-65746524
2 https://www.europarl.europa.eu/news/en/headlines/society/2023
   0601STO93804/eu-ai-act-first-regulation-on-artificial-intelligen
   ce
3 In May 2023, OpenAI's CEO Sam Altman toured European
   regulators, threatening to stop operating in Europe if the EU
   regulated AI too much (and not on his terms). https://techcrunch.
   com/2023/05/25/sam-altman-european-tour/
4 Published in March 2023, the Open Letter from the Future of Life
   Institute (and also signed by Elon Musk) claims that advanced AI
   could change the history of life on earth and get out of control,
   arguing that therefore we should pause the training of powerful AI systems for at least six months. https://futureoflife.org/
   open-letter/pause-giant-ai-experiments/

Chapter 1 Introduction

1 https://www.wsj.com/articles/white-house-warns-of-risks-as-ai
   -use-takes-off-d4cc217f
2 The website https://euraxess.ec.europa.eu/worldwide/africa/news
   /democracy-peril-commissions-ethics-group-stresses-need-and-

ways-deepen refers to a recent report on democracy in the digital age by the European Group on Ethics in Science and New Technologies (2023).

3 https://www.npr.org/2021/09/16/1037902314/the-u-n-warns-that-ai-can-pose-a-threat-to-human-rights

4 See, for example, Risse (2023) and again the letter that asked to pause the development of powerful AI.

5 By digital authoritarianism and digital totalitarianism, I mean systems of societal organization and (more broadly) control that rely on digital technologies to submit people to authority (authoritarianism) and exercise total control over them (totalitarianism). This can be done by the government but also by corporate actors. However, the main purpose of this book is not to establish and occupy this academic concept but to investigate how AI risks undermining democracy – often in ways that do not necessarily lead to authoritarianism or totalitarianism – and what can be done about it.

Chapter 2 A Not So Democratic History

1 For a nice summary of this point, see Harford (2017).

2 One could also consider some transhumanists here. While the latter's belief in the coming of humanity-surpassing technology often goes in elitist and technocratic directions, for example in the form of so-called "longtermism," some have defended a democratic version. Here the work of James Hughes is relevant: while many other transhumanists embrace libertarianism, he defends what he calls "democratic transhumanism" which is liberal, social, and democratic (Hughes 2001).

Chapter 3 What AI, What Democracy?

1 https://en.wikipedia.org/wiki/Dartmouth_workshop

2 In 1951, Alan Turing had already published a paper on a chess program. In 1997, IBM supercomputer Deep Blue won against the then world chess champion Garry Kasparov. In 2016 Google

DeepMind's AlphaGo beat Lee Sedol in the game Go. In 2022, an AI won against eight world champions at bridge.

3 Aristotle nevertheless argued in *Politics* (1998: 1276b19-30) that just as each sailor is responsible for the safety of the voyage, so each citizen is responsible for the safety of the community.

4 Note that silencing is not only and not necessarily a problem related to right-wing authoritarian tendencies. For example, Nunes Da Costa argues that today *wokeism*, cancel culture, and identity politics, which emerged in a liberal-democratic context voicing legitimate concerns about social justice, tend to become both anti-democratic and illiberal when attempting to silence people who disagree, thereby threatening fundamental democratic freedoms. I will not further discuss this claim here, but note that there are both right-wing and left-wing identity politics, and that while there surely are problematic attempts at what used to be called "censorship," it is not always clear what counts as "silencing"; it is important to distinguish between open criticism of certain views and silencing. The first is welcome in a democracy; the latter not.

5 While until recently political philosophy has been a rather anthropocentric affair, contemporary political theory has been exploring what it would mean to extend the borders of the political beyond the human. After Singer's theory of animal liberation (2009 [1975]), which rejected "speciesism" and which can be interpreted as a political theory, there have been scholars from different theoretical directions trying to include animals. For example, Donaldson and Kymlicka (2011) have discussed citizenship for animals, and Garner (2013) has proposed a theory of justice for animals. Critical posthumanists and (other) people who defend relational approaches have also questioned the anthropocentrism of traditional political theory. Some authors even consider including machines: Gunkel (2018), for example, has explored the question of robot rights.

Chapter 4 How AI Undermines the Basic Principles of Democracy

1 While at the time these principles were not applied to women, black people, and native people, this failure to universally apply them does not diminish their normative value for democracy, which requires their universal and rigorous application (an application which, depending on one's theory of justice, may include extra regard for injustices done to particular groups).

2 Puyol interprets Rawls's difference principle as an application of the principle of fraternity.

3 Note, however, that for Arendt this involved weighing one's judgment with the possible, not necessarily actual, judgments of others, in particular of humankind.

4 See also my work on AI, democracy, and epistemic agency (Coeckelbergh 2022b).

5 For example, in documents by the OECD and the European Commission.

6 Virtue epistemology is a recent approach to epistemology that can be fruitfully connected to this discussion about democracy and AI.

Chapter 5 How AI Erodes Knowledge and Trust

1 This lack of epistemic agency in turn impacts my autonomy: if I am influenced without my knowledge, then I also lack autonomy with regard to making up my mind, which Enlightenment philosophers found so important. Admittedly, epistemic agency and autonomy must be understood in a relational way: there are many influences on my beliefs due to my relation to the world and others, and therefore there is no full epistemic agency and no absolute epistemic autonomy possible. But if some degree of epistemic autonomy is not only desirable but also necessary for democracy, then if my political beliefs are manipulated by AI, there is clearly a problem of epistemic agency and autonomy, and therefore for democracy.

2 Such a right may be difficult to defend for a number of reasons

– see Risse (2023) – although one might need to put in place protections for individual epistemic agency.

3 This tends to be the case with deep-learning systems.

Chapter 6 Strengthening Democracy and Democratizing AI

1 For example, with his "common good constitutionalism," Vermeule (2022) has proposed a conservative version based on *ius commune*, in which what a flourishing political community requires is fixed. In line with the normative direction proposed in this book, a more open and dynamic constitutional order is preferred.

2 Consider, for example, privacy violations or issues concerning copyright that arise when AI is used to create texts and works of art. Here we must consider the establishment of special courts that handle tech cases. There are already many special courts; why not add one that is specialized in disputes concerning digital technologies? Moreover, given that courts and human judges are often overburdened with work, that legal support tends to be costly, and that existing legal procedures to resolve conflicts are not always very effective, efficient, and easy to understand for most citizens, AI and digital technologies themselves also offer opportunities for alternative ways of conflict resolution, for example, for mediation and dispute settlement. There are already online and algorithmic dispute resolution systems that present themselves as alternatives to going to court. This relieves some of the burden on the courts and, more importantly, helps to increase access to legal solutions for citizens. If done well, it can also enhance transparency. Both access to law and transparency are good for democracy. But here, too, there is the risk of technocracy, in particular the promotion of a kind of algorithmic approach to applying the law that is insufficiently sensitive to the unique features of the case and fails to take into account the personal experience of people – all of which is already a problem

in the current juridical system where people might be tempted to work their way through cases in an "algorithmic" way, but which may be aggravated if the process is delegated to machines. For example, Alessa (2022) has argued that AI-based systems can fail to take into account citizens' emotional responses. Such limitations undermine citizens' trust in the system, and thereby can pose a danger to the democratic and legal system as a whole and to the success of AI in society. If used in court, judges might also rely too much on automation, without using their own judgment. There is also the problem that the juridical leg of the system may become too powerful in relation to democratically elected bodies. This has always been a danger in democracies, but in the absence of a sufficient degree of tech regulation, problems with AI are likely to land on the desk of a judge rather than getting discussed by members of a democratic body.

3 See https://www.whitehouse.gov/ostp/ai-bill-of-rights/
4 See https://eur-lex.europa.eu/legal-content/EN/TXT/?uri=CEL EX:52021PC0206
5 https://eur-lex.europa.eu/legal-content/EN/TXT/?uri=celex %3A52021PC0206
6 https://www.europarl.europa.eu/news/en/headlines/society/20 230601STO93804/eu-ai-act-first-regulation-on-artificial-intelli gence
7 https://unesdoc.unesco.org/ark:/48223/pf0000381137
8 Philosophically, such a more global approach can be supported by both Hobbesian (Sætra 2022) and non-Hobbesian (Coeckelbergh 2021) arguments. Hobbes famously justified government by saying that otherwise people would find themselves in a state of nature that is nasty and brutish; in order to avoid conflict, a state authority is needed, which takes away freedom from the people but provides security and peace. Similarly, one could argue that today we find ourselves in a state of nature with regard to technology regulation at the global level: each nation-state does what it wants. This creates a dangerous, risky situation with regard to the ethical and political effects of technology. In

response, one could argue, we need a global authority that can implement effective regulation. The problem with the Hobbesian approach, however, is that it is authoritarian. We need a democratic system of global governance of technologies. In my book *Green Leviathan* (2021), I discuss this tension between freedom and authority/authoritarianism in the context of climate change and AI, and in ways that take the problem formulation beyond Hobbes.

9 See UNESCO (2021).

10 The agenda is updated regularly and can be accessed at: https://www.coe.int/en/web/artificial-intelligence/work-in-progress #01EN

11 Recently, the term "democracy by design" has also been proposed by the European Group on Ethics in Science and New Technologies in their report on democracy in the digital age (2023).

12 In the 1960s, Hofstadter complained about anti-intellectualism in the United States. In (post-?)Trump America, ignorance and anti-intellectualism pervade public life (Beres 2017).

Chapter 7 AI for Democracy and a New Renaissance

1 Note that digital humanism should not be confused with digital humanities: the latter is the study of humanities with digital methods. Digital humanities can be part of the project of digital humanism, of course, for example by helping to connect humanities to the technical disciplines.

2 There are not only humans on this planet, and non-humans also have interests. The classical humanist approach needs to be supplemented with a posthumanist sensitivity and awareness of a more holistic ecological and planetary perspective. Similarly, the Enlightenment ideals should not only protect humans. While the project of extending politics and democracy to non-humans clearly raises philosophical challenges (for example, non-human animals cannot participate in deliberation), we should at least explore what freedom, equality, justice, and democracy mean

once we become fully aware of the relational nature of humanity and the value of non-humans and their environments. This
perspective could then inform democratic AI development and,
more generally, democratic development of digital technologies.

Chapter 8 The Common Good and Communication

1 See the *Federalist Papers* No. 57, https://avalon.law.yale.edu/18
 th_century/fed57.asp
2 Kitcher (2011), by contrast, refers to Dewey but focuses on ideal
 rather than real endorsement.
3 For example, Cohen (2009) has developed an account that tries to
 integrate some notion of truth.
4 I refer here to Grotius's *Mare Liberum*: he argued for not privat-
 izing the high seas. For more discussion, see Risse (2023).
5 The phrase "tragedy of the commons" can be found in Hardin's
 famous *Science* article (1968). He gives the example of a pasture
 that is overgrazed because it is open to all and therefore each
 herder adds more and more animals. As Ostrom (1990) points
 out, Aristotle already observed in his *Politics* that what is common
 is not cared for since everyone thinks of their own interests instead
 of the common interest.
6 Note, for instance, that OpenAI first developed its AI technology
 as "open" technology but then changed its approach.
7 See, for example, https://opendatacommons.org and https://
 creativecommons.org/

References

Alessa, H. (2022). "The Role of Artificial Intelligence in Online Dispute Resolution: A Brief and Critical Overview." *Information & Communications Technology Law* 31(3): 319–42.

Allhutter, D., Cech, F., Fischer, F., Grill, G., and Mager, A. (2020). "Algorithmic Profiling of Job Seekers in Austria: How Austerity Politics are Made Effective." *Frontiers in Big Data* 3(5). https://www.frontiersin.org/articles/10.3389/fdata.2020.00005/full

Arendt, H. (1968). *Between Past and Future: Eight Exercises in Political Thought*. Penguin Books.

Arendt, H. (1998 [1958]). *The Human Condition*, 2nd edn. University of Chicago Press.

Arendt, H. (2006 [1963]). *Eichmann in Jerusalem: A Report on the Banality of Evil*. Penguin.

Arendt, H. (2017 [1951]). *The Origins of Totalitarianism*. Penguin.

Arguedas, A. R., Robertson, C. T., Fletcher, R., and Nielsen, R. K. (2022). "Echo Chambers, Filter Bubbles, and Polarisation: A Literature Review." Reuters Institute for the Study of Journalism. https://reutersinstitute.politics.ox.ac.uk/echo-chambers-filter-bubbles-and-polarisation-literature-review

Aristotle. (1998). *Politics*, ed. C. D. C. Reeve. Hackett Publishing Company.

Bacon, F. (1999 [1626]). "New Atlantis," in Susan Bruce (ed.), *Three Early Modern Utopias*. Oxford University Press.

Barker, Joshua (2015). "Guerilla Engineers," in Sheila Jasanoff and Sang Hyun-Kim (eds), *Dreamscapes of Modernity*. University of Chicago Press, pp. 199–218.

Bartoletti, I. (2020). *An Artificial Revolution*. Indigo.

Beckert, J. (2016). *Imagined Futures*. Harvard University Press.

Beckman, L. and Rosenberg, J. H. (2017). "Freedom as Non-Domination and Democratic Inclusion." *Res Publica* 24: 181–98.

Berendt, B. (2019). "AI for the Common Good?! Pitfalls, Challenges, and Ethics Pen-testing." *Paladyn, Journal of Behavioral Robotics* 10(1): 44–65. https://doi.org/10.1515/pjbr-2019-0004

Beres, L. R. (2017). "Trump's America: Anti-Intellectual and Proud of It." *YaleGlobal Online*, 17 October. https://archive-yaleglobal .yale.edu/content/trumps-america-anti-intellectual-and-proud-it

Bezzaoui, I., Fegert, J., and Weinhardt, C. (2022). "Distinguishing Between Truth and Fake: Using Explainable AI to Understand and Combat Online Disinformation," in Olga Levina, Lasse Berntzen, and Samantha Papavasiliou (eds), *Proceedings of the 16th International Conference on Digital Society (ICDS 2022)*. International Academy Research and Industry Association (IARIA).

Bimber, B. and de Zúñiga, H. Gil (2020). "The Unedited Public Sphere." *New Media & Society* 22(4): 700–15.

Blum, C. (2016). "Determining the Common Good: A (Re-) Constructive Critique of the Proceduralist Paradigm." *Phenomenology and Mind* 3: 140–8.

Bostrom, N. (2014). *Superintelligence*. Oxford University Press.

Braidotti, R. (2019). *Posthuman Knowledge*. Polity Press.

Brevini, B. (2022). *Is AI Good for the Planet?* Polity Press.

Brown, L. (2020). "Using Technology to Defeat Democracy," in James P. Steyer (ed.), *Which Side of History? How Technology is Reshaping Democracy and Our Lives.* Common Sense Media.

Cadwalladr, C. and Graham-Harrison, E. (2018). "Revealed: 50 Million Facebook Profiles Harvested for Cambridge Analytica in

Major Data Breach." *Guardian*, 17 March. https://www.theguar dian.com/news/2018/mar/17/cambridge-analytica-facebook-influ ence-us-election

China's Algorithms of Repression (2019). "Human Rights Watch." https://www.hrw.org/report/2019/05/01/chinas-algorithms -repression/reverse-engineering-xinjiang-police-mass

Coeckelbergh, M. (2021). *Green Leviathan or the Poetics of Political Liberty: Navigating Freedom in the Age of Climate Change and Artificial Intelligence.* Routledge.

Coeckelbergh, M. (2022a). *The Political Philosophy of AI: An Introduction.* Polity Press.

Coeckelbergh, M. (2022b). "Democracy, Epistemic Agency, and AI: Political Epistemology in Times of Artificial Intelligence." *AI & Ethics.* https://doi.org/10.1007/s43681-022-00239-4

Cohen, J. (1986). "An Epistemic Conception of Democracy." *Ethics* 97(1): 26–38.

Cohen, J. (2009). "Truth and Public Reason." *Philosophy and Public Affairs* 37(1): 1–42.

Coleman, S. (2017). *Can the Internet Strengthen Democracy?* Polity Press.

Couldry, N. and Meijas, U. A. (2020). *The Cost of Connection.* Stanford University Press.

Council of Europe (2020). "AI and Control of Covid-19 Coronavirus." https://www.coe.int/en/web/artificial-intelligence/ai-and-control -of-covid-19-coronavirus

Crawford, K. (2021). *Atlas of AI.* Yale University Press.

Democracy Report 2022 (2022). V-Dem Institute. https://v-dem.net /media/publications/dr_2022.pdf

Dewey, J. (1944). *Democracy and Education.* The Free Press.

Dobber, T. et al. (2021). "Do (Microtargeted) Deepfakes Have Real Effects on Political Attitudes?" *International Journal of Press/ Politics* 26(1): 69–91.

Donaldson, S. and Kymlicka, W. (2011). *Zoopolis: A Political Theory of Animal Rights.* Oxford University Press.

Dreyfus, H. (1972). *What Computers Can't Do.* MIT Press.

Duberry, J. (2022). *Artificial Intelligence and Democracy: Risks and Promises of AI-Mediated Citizen–Government Relations.* Edward Elgar Publishing.

Dulong de Rosnay, M. and Stalder, F. (2020). "Digital Commons." *Internet Policy Review* 9(4). https://doi.org/10.14763/2020.4.1 530

Durkheim, E. (1997 [1897]). *Suicide: A Study in Sociology,* trans. J. A. Spaulding and G. Simpson. The Free Press.

Dyer-Witheford, N., Mikkola Kjosen, A., and Steinhoff, J. (2019). *Inhuman Power.* Pluto Press.

Erlanger, S. (2022). "Democracy under Siege from Autocrats, Social Media and Its Own Failures." *New York Times,* 27 May. https://www.nytimes.com/2022/09/27/world/europe/democracy-politics-threats.html

Estlund, D. (2009). "Epistemic Proceduralism and Democratic Authority," in *Does Truth Matter?* Springer, pp. 15–27.

European Group on Ethics in Science and New Technologies (EGE). (2023). *Opinion on Democracy in the Digital Age.* European Commission, June 2023. https://op.europa.eu/en/web/eu-law-and-publications/publication-detail/-/publication/8b11a1bc-0f21-11ee-b12e-01aa75ed71a1

Feenberg, A. and Hannay, A. (1995). *Technology and the Politics of Knowledge.* Indiana University Press.

Feldstein, S. (2019a). "The Global Expansion of AI Surveillance." Carnegie Endowment for International Peace, 17 September. https://carnegieendowment.org/2019/09/17/global-expansion-of-ai-surveillance-pub-79847

Feldstein, S. (2019b). "The Road to Digital Unfreedom: How Artificial Intelligence is Reshaping Repression." *Journal of Democracy* 30(1): 40–52.

Fischli, R. (2022). "Data-owning Democracy: Citizen Empowerment through Data Ownership." *European Journal of Political Theory.* https://doi.org/10.1177/14748851221110316

Fletcher, R. (2020). "The Truth behind Filter Bubbles: Bursting Some Myths." Reuters Institute for the Study of Journalism, 24 January.

https://reutersinstitute.politics.ox.ac.uk/news/truth-behind-filter
-bubbles-bursting-some-myths

Floridi, L. and Cowls, J. (2019). "A Unified Framework of Five Principles for AI in Society." *Harvard Data Science Review*. https:// doi.org/10.1162/99608 f92.8cd55 0d1.

Foucault, M. (1980). *Power/Knowledge: Selected Interviews and Other Writings, 1972–79*, ed. C. Gordon. Pantheon.

Friedman, B. and Hendry, D. G. (2019). *Value Sensitive Design: Shaping Technology with Moral Imagination*. MIT Press.

Fuchs, C. (2023). *Digital Democracy and the Digital Public Sphere*. Routledge.

Garner, R. (2013). *A Theory of Justice for Animals: Animal Rights in a Nonideal World*. Oxford University Press.

Głowacka, D., Youngs, R., Pintea, A., and Wołosik, E. (2021). "Digital Technologies as a Means of Repression and Social Control." Study requested by the DROI subcommittee of European Parliament. https://www.europarl.europa.eu/RegData/etudes/STUD/2021/65 3636/EXPO_STU(2021)653636_EN.pdf

Graeber, D. and Wengrow, D. (2021). *The Dawn of Everything: A New History of Humanity*. Penguin/Allen Lane.

Greene, L. (2018). *Silicon States*. Counterpoint Press.

Guerrero, A. A. (2014). "Against Elections: The Lottocratic Alternative." *Philosophy & Public Affairs* 42(2): 135–78.

Gunkel, D. (2018). *Robot Rights*. MIT Press.

Gunn, H. and Lynch, M. P. (2021). "The Internet and Epistemic Agency," in Jennifer Lackey (ed.), *Applied Epistemology*. Oxford University Press, pp. 389–409.

Habermas, J. (1984). *The Theory of Communicative Action*. Vol. 1, trans. T. McCarthy. Beacon.

Habermas, J. (1990). *Moral Consciousness and Communicative Action*, trans. C. Lenhart and S. W. Nicholson. MIT Press.

Habermas, J. (1991). *The Structural Transformation of the Public Sphere: An Inquiry into a Category of Bourgeois Society*. MIT Press.

Harari, Y. (2015). *Sapiens: A Brief History of Humankind*. Harper.

Haraway, D. (1991). "A Cyborg Manifesto: Science, Technology, and Socialist-feminism in the Late Twentieth Century," in *Simians, Cyborgs and Women: The Reinvention of Nature*. Routledge, pp. 149–81.

Hardin, G. (1968). "The Tragedy of the Commons." *Science* 162: 1243–8.

Harford, T. (2017). "The Earliest Accountants Were the True Authors of Writing." *Accounting and Business*. https://www.accaglobal.com/my/en/member/member/accounting-business/2017/10/insights/cuneiform-writing.html

Hawley, J. (2021). *The Tyranny of Big Tech*. Regnery Publishing.

Hedlund, M. and Persson, E. (2022). "Expert Responsibility in AI Development." *AI & Society*. https://doi.org/10.1007/s00146-022-01498-9

Helbing, D. et al. (2017). "Will Democracy Survive Big Data and Artificial Intelligence?" *Scientific American*, 25 February 2017. https://www.scientificamerican.com/article/will-democracy-survive-big-data-and-artificial-intelligence/

Helmus, T. (2022). *Artificial Intelligence, Deepfakes and Disinformation: A Primer*. www.jstor.org/stable/resrep42027

Henley, J. and Booth, R. (2020). "Welfare Surveillance System Violates Human Rights, Dutch Court Rules." *Guardian*, 5 February. https://www.theguardian.com/technology/2020/feb/05/welfare-surveillance-system-violates-human-rights-dutch-court-rules

Himmelreich, J. (2022). "Against Democratizing AI." *AI & Society*. https://doi.org/10.1007/s00146-021-01357-z

Hosseinmardi, H. (2022). "It's Not Just Social Media: Cable News Has Bigger Effect on Polarization." *Ars Technica*, 10 August. https://arstechnica.com/science/2022/08/its-not-just-social-media-cable-news-has-bigger-effect-on-polarization/

House of Lords (2018). "AI in the UK: Ready, Willing and Able?" *HOUSE OF LORDS Select Committee on Artificial Intelligence Report of Session 2017–2019*. https://publications.parliament.uk/pa/ld201719/ldselect/ldai/100/100.pdf

HR-inform (n.d.). "Uber Sued over 'Robo-firing' Algorithms." https://www.hr-inform.co.uk/news-article/uber-sued-over-robo-firing-al gorithms#

Hughes, J. (2001). "The Politics of Transhumanism." http://www.changesurfer.com/Acad/TranshumPolitics.htm#_ftn2

Hussain, W. (2018). "The Common Good," in Edward N. Zalta and Uri Nodelman (eds), *The Stanford Encyclopedia of Philosophy*, Spring 2018 edn. https://plato.stanford.edu/archives/spr2018/entries/common-good/

Kant, I. (2006 [1784]). "An Answer to the Question: What is Enlightenment?" in Pauline Kleingeld (ed.), *Toward Perpetual Peace and Other Writings on Politics, Peace, and History*. Yale University Press, pp. 17–23.

Kaplan, J. (2016). *Artificial Intelligence: What Everyone Needs to Know*. Oxford University Press.

Kaspersen, A. and Wallach, W. (2023). "Now is the Moment for a Systemic Reset of AI and Technology Governance." *Carnegie Council*, 24 January. https://www.carnegiecouncil.org/media/artic le/systemic-reset-ai-technology-governance

Katyal, S. K. (2022). "Democracy & Distrust in an Era of Artificial Intelligence." *Daedalus*, 151(2): 322–34. https://www.jstor.org/st able/10.2307/48662045

Kemeny, R. (2020). "Brazil is Sliding into Techno-authoritarianism." *MIT Technology Review*, 19 August. https://www.technology review.com/2020/08/19/1007094/brazil-bolsonaro-data-privacy-cadastro-base/

Kemp, S. (2023). "Facebook Statistics and Trends." *Datareportal*, 19 February. https://datareportal.com/essential-facebook-stats

Kendall-Taylor, A., Frantz, E., and Wright, J. (2020). "The Digital Dictators: How Technology Strengthens Autocracy." *Foreign Affairs*, March/April 2020. https://www.foreignaffairs.com/articl es/china/2020-02-06/digital-dictators

Kitcher, P. (2011). *Science in a Democratic Society*. Prometheus Books.

König, P. D. and Wenzelburger, G. (2020). "Opportunity for Renewal or Disruptive Force? How Artificial Intelligence Alters Democratic Politics." *Government Information Quarterly* 37(1): 1–11.

Koster, R., et al. (2022). "Human-centred Mechanism Design with Democratic AI." *Nature Human Behaviour.* https://doi.org/10.10 38/s41562-022-01383-x

Landemore, H. (2017). "Beyond the Fact of Disagreement? The Epistemic Turn in Deliberative Democracy." *Social Epistemology* 31(3): 277–95.

Landemore, H. (2020). *Open Democracy.* Princeton University Press.

Larsen, J., Mattu, S., Kirchner, L., and Angwin, J. (2016). "How We Analyzed the COMPAS Recidivism Algorithm." *ProPublica*, May 23. https://www.propublica.org/article/how-we-analyzed-the-compas-recidivism-algorithm

Latour, B. (1983). "Give Me a Laboratory and I Will Raise the World," in Karin D. Knorr-Cetina and Michael Mulkay (eds), *Science Observed: Perspectives on the Social Studies of Science.* Sage.

Latour, B. (2002). "Morality and Technology: The End of the Means." *Theory, Culture & Society* 19(5/6): 247–26.

Latour, B. (2004). *Politics of Nature: How to Bring the Sciences into Democracy.* Harvard University Press.

Le Masurier, J. (2019). "'Our Democracy is under Threat,' Former Cambridge Analytica Employee Tells FRANCE 24." *FRANCE 24*, 28 November. https://www.france24.com/en/20191128-inter view-brittany-kaiser-cambridge-analytica-targeted-ads-facebook -democracy-under-threat

Lessig, L. (2001). *The Future of Ideas: The Fate of the Commons in a Connected World.* Random House.

Levitsky, S. and Ziblatt, D. (2018). *How Democracies Die.* Crown.

Lin, B. and Lewis, S. (2022). "The One Thing Journalistic AI Just Might Do for Democracy." *Digital Journalism.* https://doi.org/10 .1080/21670811.2022.2084131

Marx, K. and Engels, F. (2014 [1864]). *Marx and Engels's "German Ideology Manuscripts": Presentation and Analysis of the "Feuerbach Chapter."* Palgrave Macmillan.

Mazzucato, M. (2018). "Let's Make Private Data into a Public Good." *MIT Technology Review.* https://www.technologyreview.com/s/61 1489/lets-make-private-data-into-a-public-good/

Meek, A. (2020). "Minnesota is Now Using Contact Tracing to Track Protestors, as Demonstrations Escalate." *BGR*, 30 May. https:// bgr.com/lifestyle/minnesota-protest-contact-tracing-used-to-track-demonstrators/

Meikle, G. (2022). *Deepfakes.* Polity Press.

Mill, J. S. (1978 [1859]). *On Liberty.* Hackett Publishing.

Mittelstadt, B. (2019). "Principles Alone Cannot Guarantee Ethical AI." *Nature Machine Intelligence* 1: 501–7.

Mittelstadt, B., Wachter, S., and Russell, C. (2023). "The Unfairness of Fair Machine Learning: Levelling Down and Strict Egalitarianism by Default." Preprint. https://arxiv.org/ftp/arxiv/papers/2302/23 02.02404.pdf

Mouffe, C. (2013). *Agonistics: Thinking the World Politically.* Verso.

Mozur, P., Xiao, M., and Liu, J. (2022). "'An Invisible Cage': How China is Policing the Future." *The New York Times*, 25 June. https://www.nytimes.com/2022/06/25/technology/china-surveil lance-police.html

Muldoorn, J. (2022). "Data-Owning Democracy or Digital Socialism?" *Critical Review of International Social and Political Philosophy.* https://doi.org/10.1080/13698230.2022.2120737

Nemitz, P. (2018). "Constitutional Democracy and Technology in the Age of Artificial Intelligence." *Philosophical Transactions: Mathematical, Physical and Engineering Sciences* 376: 1–14.

Nguyen, C. T. (2020). "Echo Chambers and Epistemic Bubbles." *Episteme* 17(2): 141–61.

Nida-Rümelin, J. (2022). "Digital Humanism and the Limits of Artificial Intelligence," in Hannes Werthner et al. (eds), *Perspectives on Digital Humanism.* Springer.

Nunes Da Costa, M. (2022). *Democratic Despotisms.* Cambridge Scholars.

O'Neil, C. (2016). *Weapons of Math Destruction: How Big Data Increases Inequality and Threatens Democracy.* Broadway Books.

Ostrom, E. (1990). *Governing the Commons: The Evolution of Institutions for Collective Action: The Political Economy of Institutions and Decisions.* Cambridge University Press.

Owen, R., Macnaghten, P., and Stilgoe, J. (2012). "Responsible Research and Innovation: From Science in Society to Science for Society, with Society." *Science and Public Policy* 39(6): 751–60.

Pariser, E. (2011). *The Filter Bubble.* Penguin.

Peters, J. D. (2008). "Communication: History of the Idea." *International Encyclopedia of Communication.* https://onlinelibra ry.wiley.com/doi/10.1002/9781405186407.wbiecc075

Pettit, P. (1997). *Republicanism: A Theory of Freedom and Government.* Clarendon Press.

Pettit, P. (2004). "The Common Good," in Keith Dowding, Robert E. Goodin, and Carole Pateman (eds), *Justice and Democracy: Essays for Brian Barry.* Cambridge University Press, pp. 150–69.

Plato (1997) *Republic,* in John M. Cooper (ed.), *Plato: Complete Works.* Hackett, pp. 971–1223.

Popper, K. (1995 [1945]). *The Open Society and its Enemies (Vol. 1: The Spell of Plato).* Routledge.

Porter, J. (2020). "A Black Man Was Wrongfully Arrested because of Facial Recognition." *The Verge,* 24 June. https://www.theverge .com/2020/6/24/21301759/facial-recognition-detroit-police-wro ngful-arrest-robert-williams-artificial-intelligence

Putnam, R. D. (2020). *Bowling Alone: The Collapse and Revival of American Community,* rev. and updated edn. Simon & Schuster.

Puyol, A. (2019). *Political Fraternity: Democracy beyond Freedom and Equality.* Routledge.

Recke, M. (2017). "What is Digital Humanism?" NEXT Conference, 21 November. https://nextconf.eu/2017/11/what-is-digital-huma nism/#gref

Reijers, W., Orgad, L., and De Filippi, P. (2022). "The Rise of Cybernetic Citizenship." *Citizenship Studies.* https://doi.org/10 .1080/13621025.2022.2077567

Rennie, D. (2022). "An Uncertain Future." *Economist,* 15 October. https://www.economist.com/special-report/2022/10/10/

for-western-democracies-the-price-of-avoiding-a-clash-with-china-is-rising

Risse, M. (2023). *Political Theory of the Digital Age*. Cambridge University Press.

Robertson, H. and Travaglia, J. (2015). "Big Data Problems We Face Today Can be Traced to the Social Ordering Practices of the Nineteenth Century." https://blogs.lse.ac.uk/impactofsocialscien ces/2015/10/13/ideological-inheritances-in-the-data-revolution/

Robinson, S. C. (2020). "Trust, Transparency, and Openness: How Inclusion of Cultural Values Shapes Nordic National Public Policy Strategies for Artificial Intelligence (AI)." *Technology in Society* 63. https://doi.org/10.1016/j.techsoc.2020.101421

Rousseau, J.-J. (1992 [1755]). *Discourse on the Origin of Inequality*. Hackett Publishing.

Rousseau, J.-J. (1997 [1762]). "Of the Social Contract," in Victor Gourevitch (ed.), *The Social Contract and Other Later Political Writings*. Cambridge University Press, pp. 39–152.

Sætra, H. S. (2022). "A Hobbesian Argument for World Government." *Philosophies* 7(3): 66.

Sætra, H. S., Borgebund, H., and Coeckelbergh, M. (2022). "Avoid Diluting Democracy by Algorithms." *Nature Machine Intelligence*. https://doi.org/10.1038/s42256-022-00537-w

Sanders, N. E. and Schneier, B. (2023). "How ChatGPT Hijacks Democracy." *New York Times*, 15 January. https://www.nytimes .com/2023/01/15/opinion/ai-chatgpt-lobbying-democracy.html

Savaget, P., Chiarini, T. and Evans, S. (2019). "Empowering Political Participation through Artificial Intelligence." *Science and Public Policy* 46(3): 369–80. https://doi.org/10.1093/scipol/scy064

Scholz, T. (2017). "'Platform Cooperativism.' vs. the Sharing Economy," in Nicolas Douay and Annie Wan (eds), *Big Data & Civic Engagement*. Planum Publisher, pp. 47–52.

Sellers, M. N. S. (2015). "Republicanism: Philosophical Aspects", in Neil J. Smelser and Paul B. Baltes (eds), *International Encyclopedia of the Social & Behavioral Sciences*. Elsevier, pp. 477–82.

Shabaz, A. (2018). *The Rise of Digital Authoritarianism*. Freedom

House. https://freedomhouse.org/report/freedom-net/2018/rise-digital-authoritarianism

Singer, P. (2009 [1975]). *Animal Liberation*. HarperCollins.

Skinner, Q. (2008). "Freedom as the Absence of Arbitrary Power," in Cecile Laborde and John Maynor (eds), *Republicanism and Political Theory*. Blackwell Publishing, pp. 83–101.

Smith, R. E. (2019). "My Social Media Feeds Look Different from Yours and It's Driving Political Polarization." *USA Today*, 2 September. https://eu.usatoday.com/story/opinion/voices/2019/09/02/social-media-election-bias-algorithms-diversity-column/2121233001/

Splichal, S. (2022a). *Datafication of Public Opinion and the Public Sphere: How Extraction Replaced Expression of Opinion*. Anthem Press.

Splichal, S. (2022b). "In Data We (Don't) Trust: The Public Adrift in Data-Driven Public Opinion Models." *Big Data & Society*. January–June, pp. 1–13.

Starke, C., Baleis, J., Keller, B., and Marcinkowski, F. (2022). "Fairness Perceptions of Algorithmic Decision-making: A Systematic Review of the Empirical Literature." *Big Data & Society* 9(2). https://doi.org/10.1177/20539517221115189

Sudmann, A. (ed.) (2019). *The Democratization of Artificial Intelligence: Net Politics in the Era of Learning Algorithms*. Transcript Verlag.

Susskind, J. (2022). *The Digital Republic: On Freedom and Democracy in the 21st Century*. Bloomsbury.

Tang, A. (2019). "Inside Taiwan's New Digital Democracy." *Economist*, 12 May. https://www.economist.com/open-future/2019/03/12/inside-taiwans-new-digital-democracy

Taylor, C. (1985). "Alternative Futures: Legitimacy, Identity and Alienation in Late Twentieth Century Canada," in Alan Cairns and Cynthia Williams (eds), *Constitutionalism, Citizenship, and Society in Canada*. University of Toronto Press, pp. 183–229.

de Tocqueville, A. (2012 [1835]). *Democracy in America*. Liberty Fund.

Turing, A. (1950). "Computing Machinery and Intelligence." *Mind*

49(236): 433–60. https://redirect.cs.umbc.edu/courses/471/papers/turing.pdf

UNESCO (2021). "Recommendation on the Ethics of Artificial Intelligence." https://unesdoc.unesco.org/ark:/48223/pf0000381137

Van Den Hoven, J. (2013). "Value Sensitive Design and Responsible Innovation," in Richard Owen, John Bessant, and Maggy Heintz (eds), *Responsible Innovation*. John Wiley & Sons, pp. 75–83.

Véliz, C. (2020). *Privacy is Power*. Bantam Press.

Verbeek, P. P. (2011). *Moralizing Technology*. Chicago University Press.

Vermeule, A. (2022). *Common Good Constitutionalism*. Polity Press.

Voltaire (1962 [1764]). *Philosophical Dictionary*. Basic Books.

Von Schomberg, R. (2013). "A Vision of Responsible Research and Innovation," in Richard Owen, John Bessant, and Maggy Heintz (eds), *Responsible Innovation*. Wiley, pp. 51–74.

Warburton, N. (2009). "Free Speech in the Age of the Internet," in *Free Speech: A Very Short Introduction*. Oxford University Press, pp. 81–95. https://doi.org/10.1093/actrade/9780199232352.003.0005

Werthner, H., Prem, E., Lee, E. A., and Ghezzi, C. (2022). *Perspectives on Digital Humanism*. Springer. https://link.springer.com/book/10.1007/978-3-030-86144-5

Wiener, N. (1948). *Cybernetics: Or, Control and Communication in the Animal and the Machine*. MIT Press.

Winner, L. (1986). "Do Artifacts Have Politics?" in *The Whale and the Reactor: A Search for Limits in an Age of High Technology*. University of Chicago Press, pp. 19–39.

Zarkadakis, G. (2020). *Cyber Republic: Reinventing Democracy in the Age of Intelligent Machines*. MIT Press.

Zeng, J. (2020). "Artificial Intelligence and China's Authoritarian Governance." *International Affairs* 96(6): 1441–59.

Zuboff, S. (2015). "Big Other: Surveillance Capitalism and the Prospects of an Information Civilization." *Journal of Information Technology* 30(1): 75–89.

Zuboff, S. (2019). *The Age of Surveillance Capitalism*. Profile Books.

Index

Printed and bound by CPI Group (UK) Ltd, Croydon, CR0 4YY

16/04/2025

14658410-0003